PHOTOGRAPHY
Liverpool Record Office and Liverpool Libraries,
Liverpool Daily Post & Echo,
National Museums Liverpool,
David Cottrell, Colin Harrison
and Tracy Smith

THE POOL OF LIFE

Here we are then, eight centuries on since King John Plantagenet's autograph (or rather the impression of his seal, if we're being technical) gave birth to one of the most famous cities in the world. Anniversaries like this only come around every 100 years, but as it happens Liverpool has plenty to celebrate. It is currently undergoing a remarkable renaissance, and immediately after 2007 – Liverpool's 800th – it's European Capital of Culture.

The preceding years have been themed, too, highlighting different aspects of the city's unique culture. Celebrating Learning 2003 marked the centenary of the founding of the University of Liverpool and the 150th anniversary of the ecumenical foundation of Liverpool Hope, while with Faith in One City 2004 Liverpool emphasised its place as a multi-cultural city. Then came Sea Liverpool 2005 celebrating maritime heritage, with the city staging the 25th annual Mersey River Festival and the start of the Clipper Round the World Yacht Race and also marking the 200th anniversary of Nelson's victory at Trafalgar – a watershed that allowed Liverpool to grow and prosper into one of the most important ports in the British Empire.

Most recently Liverpool Performs 2006 marked the city's performance record in sport, art and business, with highlights like the fourth Liverpool Biennial and the Open Golf Championship.

The year 2008 promises to be Europe's biggest and most diverse celebration of culture as Liverpool takes centre stage. Then it's 2009 the Year of Environment and 2010 ushering in a Year of Innovation.

For the moment, let's stick with the here and now. Liverpool is celebrating 800 years of remarkable history, a whole programme of events is being planned, and you're holding in your hands the official souvenir brochure.

Happy reading, and have fun…

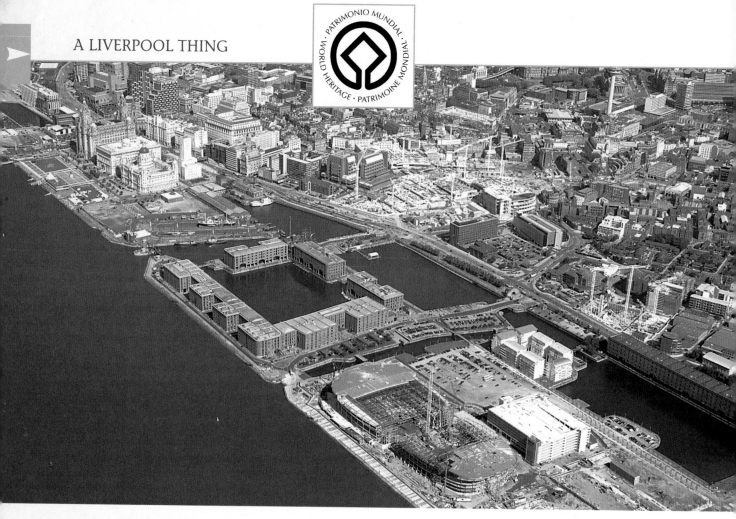

WORLD EXCLUSIVE

How 800 years of history and heritage add up to the supreme accolade

Liverpudlians always knew their home was one of the most important places on the planet, and official confirmation came with its inscription as a UNESCO World Heritage Site in 2004. Listed as a Maritime Mercantile City, it's described as 'the supreme example of a commercial port at the time of Britain's greatest global influence'.

The site's boundary includes much more than just the Pier Head and docklands. There are also those parts of the city that relate directly to its historic role as a port: the Castle Street/Dale Street commercial district where shipping offices, exchanges and banks are located; the Lower Duke Street merchants quarter where warehouses are located; and the William Brown Street cultural quarter which illustrates the ambition of 19th Century Liverpool to display civic pride and interest in cultural values as well as commercial gain, funded by profits from the maritime trade.

Tours are proving to be hugely popular with visitors, who can pick up free maps at the 08 Place and Tourist Information Centres and benefit from guided tours by the entertaining Blue Badge guides, some in period costume. And remember: unlike many

World Heritage Sites, there is no charge to enter Liverpool to admire its grandeur. There's even free admission to all of the outstanding museums and galleries under the control of National Museums Liverpool. Visit liverpoolworldheritage.com

HISTORY IN THE MAKING

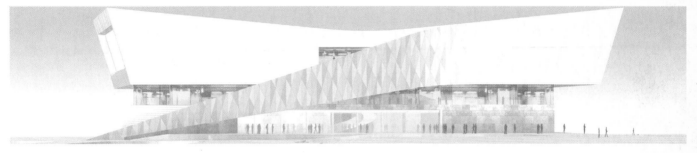

Our 800th birthday finds work underway on a monumental city milestone – the new Museum of Liverpool situated at the Pier Head. As the biggest newly-built English national museum for almost a century, it's already been hailed as 'one of the great cultural achievements in Liverpool's history'. Housed in a contemporary design to reflect its maritime location and complement its illustrious neighbours, the museum will welcome 750,000 visitors a year, with four main galleries called Port City, Global City, People's City and Creative City.

➤ A special honour in an extra-special year for Liverpool – its photographic collections have been recognised as being of international importance. The Museums, Libraries & Archives Council has awarded Liverpool Record Office the prestigious 'designation status' for its extensive archive of images.

Meanwhile, over at the Philharmonic Hall, archives dating back to the orchestra's creation are on display in 2007. The collection includes programmes, tickets and the autographs of the legendary Edward Elgar and Russian composer Rachmaninov.

Plus ça change...

Has Liverpool changed that much over the last 100 or so years? Certainly, there are some fabulous new developments complete and underway, but it seems the fabric of the city centre remains reassuringly the same. Here are some fascinating pen-and-ink pictures of Liverpool from 120 years ago. They were taken from a souvenir booklet published by Lewis's and commemorating an 'International Exhibition of Navigation, Commerce and Industry in Liverpool, England', opened by Queen Victoria herself on 11 May 1886 (the same year, incidentally, that the underground Mersey Railway opened). On the right of each picture, comparative photographs from today...

Castle Street and Town Hall: Horse-drawn carriages instead of buses, and all of the façades on the south side of Castle Street seem to have changed. Note the newer, bigger Exchange Flags that replaced the old cloistered square behind the Town Hall.

George's Landing Stage: The same Parish Church with its steeple on the left, and the same Mersey Chambers (formerly offices of the T & J Harrison shipping line) in the middle, but the Tower Building (on the right) got an Edwardian makeover in 1908.

St George's Hall: A near-enough identical vista, but the tramlines and ornate lamp standards have long gone, as has the magnificent sculptural relief in the pediment (held up by the Hall's south columns) which fell off and was used for road-building aggregate.

Brown's Museum & Picton Reading Room: Another similar view, although William Brown Street's furniture has changed over the years, with trees and balustrades now complementing the great classical buildings, and less chance these days of being run over by a horse.

WORLD IN ONE CITY

Liverpool's global heritage. A concise A-Z...

AFRICA: Underneath the viewing platform for the Piazza Waterfall at Beetham Plaza, there's a plaque in the shape of two tribal spears and a shield that commemorates the original site of the arcaded warehouses of Goree Piazza, named after an island off the coast of Senegal. The Slave Trade funded Liverpool's phenomenal growth in the 18th Century, but its original black community – the oldest in Britain – is descended from Afro-American seamen who married local women.

AMERICA: No19 Abercromby Square, now university property near Hope Quarter, was once the home of Charles Prioleau, a Confederate businessman during the American Civil War. Painted on the vestibule ceiling is a palmetto tree, the symbol of South Carolina (from 1776 when colonists in Charleston defended a fort built from palmetto logs against the British). On the ceilings of the old dining room are cherubs – one of them astride a wild turkey, the state's game-bird.

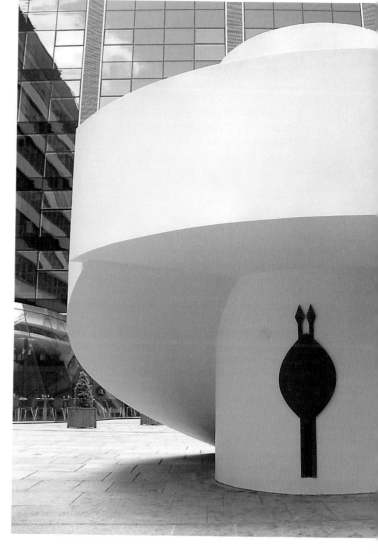

CHINA: While California attracted cheap Chinese labour to build its Central Pacific Railroad in the middle of the 19th Century, Liverpool did so for its merchant shipping. 'It is noteworthy', reported the Liverpool Courier, 'that from the earliest years of their settlement the Chinese have been regarded as the embodiment of public order'. The population reached its zenith in the 1940s when photographer Bert Hardie recorded it for the Picture Post.

LIVERPOOL FIRSTS

Liverpool's Chinese community is the oldest in Europe, originating from direct trade routes starting in 1865

CANADA: Canada Dock was opened in 1853 to handle North American timber. Liverpool had a shipping line called Canadian Pacific, and 500,000 emigrants sailed to Quebec from here.

FRANCE: Around 4,000 French prisoners were detained in Liverpool during the Napoleonic wars. Those who died were buried in what is now St John's Gardens. Legend has it, some helped to build sections of the Dock Wall around Wapping.

IRELAND: Between 1849 and 1852 over 1.2million Irish emigrants arrived in Liverpool to escape famine back home. Their contribution to the city's culture, heritage and identity is incalculable.

ISRAEL: In the mid-18th Century many Jewish refugees fleeing persecution in eastern Europe passed through Liverpool en route to North America, but at least 5,000 stayed on and the city elected its first Jewish mayor in 1863. Nine years later the Moorish Revival synagogue on Princes Road was consecrated. Today a Jewish Heritage Trail leaflet is available from Tourist Information Centres.

ITALY: Italian immigrants arrived in Liverpool between 1880 and 1912, settling in the Gerard Street area which became known as Little Italy. Boxer Dom Volante was born here in 1905 and went on to fight at New York's Madison Square Gardens.

RUSSIA: Following the Bolshevik Revolution there was an influx of Russians to Liverpool in the early 20th Century, including the families of opera singer Fyodor Chaliapin, Black Sea navy admiral Pavel Nakhimov and the tsarevitch Alexei's former nanny.

SCOTLAND: The Liverpool Scottish was formed in 1900 as an infantry battalion. Adopting the Clan Forbes tartan as part of their Highland dress uniform, they served extensively during the First World War.

WALES: Situated in Liverpool Town Hall are a couple of Bardic chairs from the last two National Eisteddfods held in the city, in 1884 and 1900. Thousands of Welsh came to Liverpool in the late 18th Century – they even had their own Welsh newspaper – and the community in Patagonia came from a clipper that left Liverpool in 1865.

Last time round...

In 1907, Liverpool celebrated its 700th birthday with fitting pomp and circumstance. At the time, the city owned one seventh of the world's shipping, with the Mersey registering a third more tonnage (over ten million) year on year and handling much bigger ships than the shallower Thames.

There was a week-long 'Anniversary Festival' featuring a Historical Procession and Tableaux, Public Thanksgiving Service, Display of Fireworks, Arrival in the Mersey of the Channel Fleet of Fourteen Battleships, and Variety Entertainments in Sefton Park, Wavertree Park, Lister Drive and Queens Drive. A Song to Liverpool was also composed and went something like this...

Hail! Queen and Goddess of our City,
Nestling on seven hills, and ruling Mersey's tides!
Strew the posies in her way; make a merry holiday;
For in triumph see! the Goddess gaily rides!

Seven Centuries have passed;
But wrinkled Time hast cast
The gleam of youthful glory on her face,
Seven oceans read her name,
bend in homage to her fame,
Rise to kiss the titled sterns with eager grace.

Not a ripple leaves her quay,
But it bears across the sea
Love's message to her children East and West,
Not a Zephir fans her cheeks;
But a tender whisper speaks
Of a loyal heart that homeward turns for rest.

Mother! Portress of the Home land!
How fare the children in the Saffron lands of dawn
I have sent them on their way,
For the labours of the day;
But Eve shall find them to my bosom drawn.

Mother! Portress of the Home land!
How fare the children, who wander on the deep
O, to serve is all their prize,
Though they gather merchandise
And they learn to sweat and toil, while others reap.

Hail! Queen and Goddess of our City,
Almoner of welcome, with the sunset in thine eyes,
Strew the posies in her way; make a merry holiday;
And proclaim her Mother, tender, true and wise.

LIVERPOOL IS...

Changing...
You can't help but notice the Big Dig – the massive transformation of Liverpool to the tune of £3billion, including the Paradise Project (biggest retail scheme of its kind in Europe), King's Waterfront (major arena and conference zone), forthcoming cruise-liner facility, and City Centre Movement Strategy (improving access all over town).

Connected...
The 08 Place in Whitechapel is a focal point for the Capital of Culture experience, providing tourist info, merchandise and a tour booking service, while the nearby Paradise Project's call-in centre on Lord Street has a huge scale model of the £800million site-well worth a gander. You'll also find a system of info panels all over the city-centre designed to make discovery easier. They feature a mapping system displaying iconic buildings in 3D and areas within six minutes' walk – all in clear colours for visually-impaired people with clear identification of steps and areas inaccessible to wheelchair users. There's a state-of-the-art Big Screen, too, at Clayton Square, operational 24 hours a day, broad-casting BBC shows as well as local info, and a very visible campaign to keep locals and visitors aware of all the transformations taking place.

LIVERPOOL IS...

Lively...

Welcome to a vibrant city centre with a growing population, raft of stylish and innovative new developments and lots of bright public spaces. The nightlife? In a word, legendary. You can't open a fashion mag without finding some mention of trend-setting store Cricket, whose catwalk shows receive national coverage. Coming very soon is the shopping paradise that is Liverpool One, while the Met Quarter is another slice of retail heaven, combining an historic frontage with innovative art and design elements inside. Thursday is late-night shopping in the city centre, with stores staying open till 8pm.

Appetising...

Peckish? Choose from at least 50 restaurants within easy reach with a breadth and variety of cuisine worthy of a cosmopolitan, 21st Century city. There's British, Argentinian French, Italian, Spanish, Portuguese, Indian, Chinese, Japanese, Thai, North American, Mexican, Chilean, Russian, Turkish and Greek. That's not counting the cafés, bistros, gastropubs, lounge bars, hotels etc. Liverpool has benefited from a regeneration of its pedestrian areas in line with the 2008 preparations, and European-style café culture is now a feature of one of its most elegant thoroughfares.

GREEN AND SERENE

Let's hear it for Liverpool's historic parks and gardens...

A big, brawny city on a windswept coastline with miles upon miles of gritty docklands – and one million trees and over 2,500 acres of parks and open spaces. The great swathes of Stanley, Newsham and Sefton Parks are a legacy from late Victorian days when Liverpool's great and good had the foresight to create green lungs and leafy arteries for a city seething with humanity. Earlier still, the city boasted magnificent Botanic Gardens, opened at Mount Pleasant by man of letters William Roscoe in 1802. After a later spell at Edge Lane, the collections were eventually dispersed to Calderstones Park and finally Garston.

Calderstones Park, Harthill entrance

Today ten parks have been awarded Green Flag status, while Chavasse Park is being re-landscaped as part of Grosvenor's Paradise Street project. There remains lots of urban retreats in town like St John's Gardens, Falkner Square, Abercromby Square, the Liverpool John Moores University Garden off Maryland Street, St James' Cemetery and the grounds of Church of Our Lady & St Nicholas.

The Council's Park Strategy for Liverpool aims to establish a Friends Group for every high-level park within three years, and 50 per cent of Scousers to live within 500 metres of a Green Flag park within a decade. All the parks can be explored with Park Rangers, who offer a wide range of walks, tours and organised events, mostly free of charge (0151 233 2008).

FAME ACADEMY

Where to find Liverpool's great and good from days gone by: John Brodie (Mersey tunnel engineer) relief outside Queensway entrance; William Brown (philanthropist) statue in St George's Hall; Dr William Duncan (first Medical Officer) pub sign on St John's Lane; George Canning (politician) statue in Town Hall; Dixie Dean (Everton FC legend) statue at Goodison Park; Billy Fury (rocker, left) statue, National Museums Liverpool ; William Gladstone (Prime Minister) statue in St John's Gardens; William Huskisson (politician) statue off Duke Street; Agnes Jones (nursing pioneer) statue in Oratory by Liverpool Cathedral; William Rathbone (slavery abolitionist) statue in St George's Hall; William Roscoe (philanthropist) pub sign on Roscoe Street; Bill Shankly (Liverpool FC legend) statue at Anfield; Kitty Wilkinson (cholera heroine) stained glass in Liverpool Cathedral.

FAB 48 HOURS

DAY ONE: At Liverpool John Lennon Airport is a statue of the great man himself, unveiled by Yoko in March 2002, and outside is the Yellow Submarine. First stop in town, the Beatles Story museum on Albert Dock with the original 60s waxworks from Madame Tussauds, George's first-ever guitar and John's orange-tinted glasses. Next up, the Town Hall balcony where thousands cheered the Fab Four before the premiere of A Hard Day's Night on 10 July 1964. On Mathew Street there's another statue of John, plus the Wall of Fame – 54 Liverpool No1 chart hits since 1952. Have a swift half in The Grapes where the boys often drank before you browse Cavern Designer Shopping Centre (designed by Cynthia Lennon) then visit the old place itself – or rather a faithful replica built on the site where, for the record, the Beatles played 292 times between 1961 and 1963.

DAY TWO: Step right this way for a Magical Mystery Tour by coach to Penny Lane, where the barber still shaves another customer, and Strawberry Fields, where John used to play. In the afternoon, take a scheduled tour to Mendips and 20 Forthlin Road, the childhood homes of John and Paul respectively. Back in town to the LIPA on Hope Street, formerly the Liverpool Insitute attended by George and Paul. Also here, the old Liverpool School of Art that numbered John and Stuart Sutcliffe among its students. On Rice Street is Ye Cracke where John formed his first band The Dissenters. Then it's last orders at old beatnik haunt the Jacaranda (Slater Street). They found murals by John here when they scrubbed the basement walls, and his ghost was allegedly seen arguing with a barmaid from 1959 called Audrey. He always was the bolshie one.

LIVERPOOL IS...

Photogenic...
Liverpool looks good, which is why so many films and TV dramas are shot here. On average the city's Film Office organises the equivalent of over 500 days of filming each year. Recent productions include the BBC's Casanova, an Elizabethan drama filmed at St George's Hall and Stanley Dock, and Alfie, starring Jude Law and featuring scenes in which Liverpool doubled as New York. The city has also stood in for the likes of Moscow and Rome.

Lyrical...
Music's been a way of life at least since the 'Cunard Yanks' – Liverpool seamen returning home from the States in the 1950s – brought back the jeans, guitars and rock 'n' roll records that spawned the Merseybeat sound and the heyday of the Cavern. After an explosion of new bands in the 80s and the gig scene centred on Eric's, there came superclub Cream, and today Liverpool's live-music scene remains as exciting and diverse as ever.

Must see must do...

➤All aboard the The Yellow Duckmarine, a 50-minute, fun-and-frolic, land-and-river tour ➤Take a dash through the new Williamson Square fountain without getting your feet or head wet ➤Ponder Jorge Pardo's Penelope (Wolstenholme Square) and engage Tracey Emin's Roman Standard (Oratory, Liverpool Cathedral) ➤Take in a movie in the second-floor cinemas at FACT and sink into their ergonomically-designed seats ➤Do Drome, Peach, Cricket and Boodle & Dunthorne (serious bling) ➤Wonder at John James Audubon's Birds of America in Central Library – one of only 133 copies of the most valuable natural history book printed ➤Sleep in style at the Radisson SAS hotel and admire its Face of Liverpool urban art project ➤Unleash your digital camera on eight Grade I listed buildings – Albert Dock, Royal Liver Building, Oriel Chambers, Town Hall, Bank of England, Bluecoat Chambers, St George's Hall and Liverpool Cathedral ➤Take an hour-long Mersey Ferries River Explorer Cruise (the Iris and Daffodil are 'Royal', because they saw action at Zeebrugge in the Great War) ➤Go modern at Tate Liverpool then peruse the collections in World Museum Liverpool ➤Catch compelling drama at the Playhouse or Everyman theatres – a great night-out guaranteed ➤Listen to smuggling stories at Merseyside Maritime Museum, plus the sights and sounds of emigration ➤Play with puppets and costumes at the Walker's Artbase every weekend and daily from mid-July to early September for the school hols ➤Explore the beauty of Speke Hall.

making history

1207
John proclaims that 'all who have taken burgage houses at Lyrpul shall have all the liberties and free customs of the town of Lyrpul which any free borough on sea has in our territories'.

1220
Ranulph, Earl of Chester, erects Everton Beacon as a navigation guide. It lasts for 600 years.

1229
Henry III makes Liverpool a 'free borough for ever'.

1266
William de Ferrers, Earl of Derby, is deposed for treason and Liverpool is placed under the Earl of Lancaster.

1295
Early mention of John de Mora (Moore) as Liverpool's bailiff.

1307
Liverpool celebrates its 100th anniversary.

1317
Edward II grants ferry rights to the priory of Birkenhead.

1331
First reference to Liverpool on a map of Britain.

BIRTH OF A CITY. BY ROYAL APPOINTMENT
It was 800 years ago today, King John made Liverpool's day...

Difficult to conjure Liverpool Castle from the mists of medieval time. But it's only 280 years since it was demolished. In 1207, Liverpool was a small hamlet not mentioned by name in the Domesday Book. But King John needed a port of embarkation to Ireland, and Liverpool was ideal. On 28 August his charter invited settlers to come to Liverpool with certain privileges. His royal stronghold was built by William de Ferrers, overlord of Liverpool, between 1207 and 1235. It stood on a rocky headland (now Derby Square and the Victoria Monument) with the Mersey lapping at its edge (today's

Liverpool Castle

nearby Law Courts and Grosvenor's Paradise Project are on the site of a tidal creek called the Pool). The castle changed hands several times during the English Civil War but was demolished in 1726.

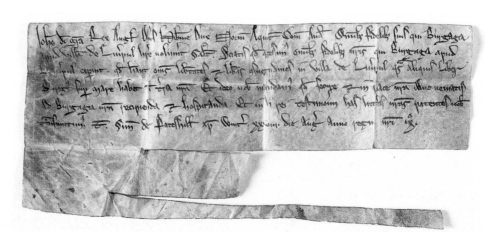

Liverpool in the 17th Century

Speke Hall

Stanleys (Earls of Derby) since 1385. It sits in 2,500 acres and houses outstanding art.

Embedded in the road surface outside the NatWest Bank on Castle Street, the Sanctuary Stone (below) marks the boundary of the old Liverpool Fairs held on 25 July and 11 November each year, when debtors were allowed to conduct lawful business free from arrest.

Speke Hall (above) is one of Britain's most famous Tudor manors, a half-timbered house set in a wooded estate with fine gardens and panoramic views over the Mersey. Built between 1490 and 1612, it was formerly owned by the Norris Family then sugar magnate Richard Watt. Croxteth Hall, ancestral home of the Molyneux (Earls of Sefton) dates from 1575. The last lord died without heirs in 1972. Knowsley Hall, Liverpool's only genuine stately home, has been owned by the

making history

1351
William de Liverpool becomes first mayor of Liverpool. A decade later, Edward III orders his navy to speed to 'Lytherpool' and Chester to prepare for an attack upon Ireland.

1379
Poll Tax returns show 26 Liverpudlians engaged in agriculture, 18 brewers, nine servants, nine cobblers, five fishmongers, four drapers, three tailors, two smiths, the mayor, a franklin (freeholder not of noble birth), tanner, butcher, carpenter, chaloner, weaver and baker.

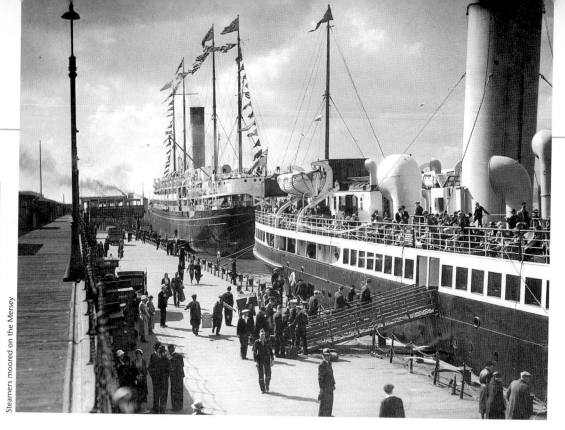

Steamers moored on the Mersey

making history

1400

The Moore family acquire the manor of Kirkdale and build a substantial residence called Bank Hall. Five years later the Stanley family are granted lordship of the Isle of Man 'forever' and build a stronghold at the foot of Water Street.

1407

Liverpool celebrates its 200th anniversary.

1425

Liverpool's most powerful families, the Molyneux and Stanleys, avoid open warfare only with the intervention of the Sheriff of Lancaster.

1485

The Stanleys take the title Earl of Derby, for their role at the Battle of Bosworth.

1507

Liverpool's prosperity increases during the Tudor dynasty. Celebrates its 300th anniversary.

1515

First Town Hall built in Dale Street, by John Crosse. Acts as court and exchange.

1540

Town heavily afflicted by plague. Seven years later there are just four ships in port.

THRESHOLD TO THE ENDS OF THE EARTH
This great city has saltwater running through its veins...

A mile-wide stretch of muddy water – for the quality of Mersey is not strained – mirrors the weather of the day, now deep, turgid and impenetrable like the cloak of encircling grey cloud, now sprightly dancing with tufts of white blown spray as the clear sky throws up a translucent brilliance with follows a northern wind...' (Quentin Hughes, 1964).

This is Liverpool, this is the sea. Like love and marriage, you can't have one without the other. The place is defined by its location, looking out and away. The Mersey, declared writer Michael O'Mahoney in 1931, 'is a threshold to the ends of the earth', assisted by the great shipping lines of Cunard, White Star and P&O.

The Pier Head remains the focal point, but it was from Princes Dock – after the slave trade – that millions of emigrants left for the New World while its cargoes came the other way. Inland and opposite the historic Albert Dock is today's massive

Paradise Project – 150 years ago a warren of streets nicknamed Sailortown and crammed with drinking dens with names like the Ship Inn and Black Dog Tavern.

Running for six miles is the 200-year-old Dock Wall, rising 18ft high in places. The novelist Nathaniel Hawthorne, American consul in Liverpool in the 1850s, likened it to the Great Wall of China. Similarly, an overhead railway – dubbed the Docker's Umbrella – once ran the length of this area until its demolition in 1956.

⚑ LIVERPOOL FIRSTS

The Albert Dock, devised by the great Jesse Hartley, is the largest group of Grade I listed buildings in the country

LIVERPOOL FIRSTS

Liverpool's 'Old Dock' was constructed in 1715 as the world's first enclosed wet dock. Recent excavations have revealed its walls

LIVERPOOL
1207~2007

OFFICIAL SOUVENIR

The Juan Sebastian De Elcano on the Mersey, painted by ED Walker

Clippers in Salthouse Dock

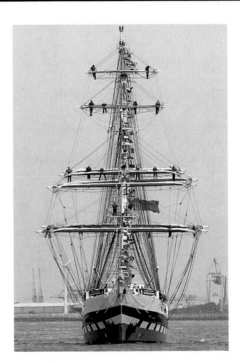

making history

1565
Liverpool has 138 householders, with a population of about 690. The port consists of ten barques and two boats employing 75 men and carrying goods between Ireland, Wales and the Isle of Man and Liverpool.

1570
Liverpool ships exporting coal, iron, copper, hops, cloth and soap, and importing tallow, linen, flax, wool, salt herrings and beef.

1592
Ancient Royal Park of Toxteth was broken up and divided into farms for Puritans.

1607
Population of Liverpool estimated at 2,000. Celebrates its 400th anniversary.

1611
Salt works at the bottom of Chapel Street improves Liverpool's communications with its hinterland and leads to the development of canals.

1618
Puritan chapel established, with Jeremiah Horrocks a pupil. Still survives under name of the Ancient Chapel of Toxteth.

1641

Trade with West Indies begins. The Moore family seems to have some interests in ships between Barbados and Liverpool.

1642

English Civil War starts. Cavaliers (nobles and gentry) ultimately lose possession of Liverpool Castle to Parliamentarians. John Moore becomes governor of Liverpool.

1647

Liverpool becomes a free port, no longer under the rule of Chester.

1648

First reported cargo arrives from America. The ship is called Friendship, with a cargo of mainly tobacco.

1649

John Moore signs the death warrant for the execution of Charles I.

1668

Lord Molyneux lays out Lord Street. Trade from the West Indies begins to pass through Liverpool.

1674

Second Town Hall is built.

CITY OF THE SEA
The oceans set in stone...

In the carved relief above the old bank's entrance, the heraldic shield bobs upon a ripple of intricately-carved waves. On the left, Neptune grasps a frond of seaweed. To the right, a mermaid twists a strand of her own flowing, kelp-like hair in her hand. A few feet away, silhouetted against the sky high above the doors of the Marks & Spencer store, sits another Neptune embracing a coat of arms. Here his crown resembles the spines of an anemone, his deep-set eyes and wispish beard giving him a venerable, contemplative air.

Detail on Martins Bank, Water Street

Entrance gates to Port of Liverpool Building

With its iconic Pier Head landmarks and miles upon miles of docklands, this is an open gallery for epic public sculpture, invariably with a maritime theme, that takes some beating – only London surpasses the city for this most accessible of art forms.

By the beginning of the 19th Century, Liverpool's phenomenal growth – funded by the transatlantic slave trade then mercantile shipping and passenger traffic – saw vast personal fortunes amassed by a merchant class that sought to beautify their home town with decorative sculpture.

Façade of former Liverpool Union Bank, Bold Street

Neptune relief on Cunard Building, Pier Head

Carved ornament was dominated by nautical imagery like oars and rigging, scallop shells and mermaids, dolphins, seahorses, starfish and fabulous denizens of the deep. There were allegorical figures representing commerce, navigation and the River Mersey, and classical deities such as Neptune. The Greek god of the sea appears upon the city's coat of arms brandishing his trident alongside a triton blowing his conch and the mythical Liver Bird – most closely resembling a cormorant with a sprig of seaweed in its bill. The city motto, Deus Nobis Haec Otia Fecit, comes from the Eclogues of Virgil and translates as: 'These

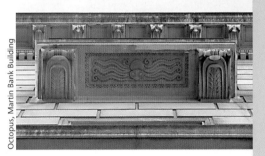

Octopus, Martin Bank Building

gifts God has bestowed upon us'.

Fabulous maritime sculpture continued well into the early 20th Century in a city that likened itself first to ancient Athens then Renaissance Venice and Florence, and finally the great American cities of Chicago and New York. The last flourish is exemplified by the colossal Martins Bank Building on Water Street. Completed in 1932 under the stewardship of chief architect Herbert Rowse, it's awash inside and out with musclebound Neptunes with splendid fish tails and fin-like girdles – 'classical motifs reduced to geometric stylisations' as one scholar puts it – and serene and voluptuous mermaids with cascades of golden hair. A glorious reminder, as the city's current renaissance continues apace, of an era when Liverpool truly ruled the waves.

Merman detail, Port of Liverpool Building

making history

1707
Liverpool acquires Customs House, giving control over its own trading affairs. Celebrates its 500th anniversary.

1715
The world's first commercial wet dock is built. Upper reaches of the Pool are drained and new streets built upon the reclaimed land.

1717
Bryan Blundell founds the Bluecoat. 'Dedicated to the promotion of Christian charity and the training of poor boys in the principles of the Anglican Church'.

1725
Chadwick instructed by the Council to produce a map of Liverpool, the first survey and measurement of the town. Two years later Liverpool Castle demolished.

1748
Liverpool Royal Infirmary built on the present site of St George's Hall.

1753
Growth of salt trade leads to building of Salthouse dock. Third Town Hall opens.

Djimon Hounsou in the film Amistad

Liverpool slaving ship by William Jackson

William Roscoe

AGAINST HUMAN DIGNITY
A baleful legacy of Liverpool's seafaring past...

In December 2006, a national broadsheet newspaper ran a feature about the descendants of slave traders, including Sir George Earle who donated his family archives to National Museums Liverpool. The Earles were a prominent Liverpool family in 18th Century Liverpool, and today's street (off Old Hall Street) is named after them. The History of the Liverpool Privateers with an Account of the Liverpool Slave Trade 1744-1812, was written by Gomer Williams, first published in 1897 and reprinted in 2004 by Liverpool University Press.

It stresses that the trade was 'not the foundation of the port's rise to major status' and 'as late as the 1780s Liverpool still lagged behind London in the number of slave trading ventures dispatched'. But it clarifies that 'by 1807, when the British traffic was abolished, Liverpool had become the leading British centre for slave trading'. It was thanks to the efforts of a brave band of men and women, black and white, that the trade was finally brought to an end. Members of the abolitionist movement often put their own lives at risk for their cause.

Maritime Museum exhibition

In Liverpool, the memory of abolitionists such as William Roscoe, William Rathbone, Daniel Daulby and John Yates lives on. On 9 December 1999 Liverpool City Council passed a formal motion apologising for the city's part in the slave trade.

It was unanimously agreed that Liverpool acknowledge its responsibility for its involvement over three centuries. While bequeathing the city a rich diversity of people and cultures, learning, architecture and financial wealth, it also obscured the human suffering upon which it was built.

The misery it caused left a legacy that affects black people in Liverpool today. The city has made International Slavery Remembrance Day (23 August) an official part of its cultural calendar.

making history

1755
Parliament passes Act to build the Sankey Canal, connecting Liverpool with the coalfields around St Helens – the first canal to be built in Britain.

1761
Liverpool's first Dock Committee is set up.

1775
Liverpool seamen attack Town Hall with canon in protest at having wages reduced. Economy in recession due to American War of Independence.

1778
Privateer ship the Mentor captures the French ship the Carnatic, yielding a profit of £135,000 for Peter Baker, who uses the money to build Carnatic Hall.

CITY WITH A THIRST FOR THE WORK ETHIC
Business, industry and engineering all take pride of place...

Tate & Lyle, Ford, Meccano, Littlewoods... Just a few of the names indelibly linked with Liverpool's working heritage. The docks, historically, were the biggest employers, and the Overhead Railway, or 'Docker's Umbrella', not only transported people and goods the length of the waterfront but also enabled many a starry-eyed youngster to view the port's great industrial expanse in all of its splendour.

For a feat of engineering, though, Queensway Road tunnel – at the time the world's longest – takes some beating. Opened in 1934, it ran from Liverpool to Birkenhead and required the excavation of 1.2million tons of rock over five years. To put it another way, one ton was removed every two minutes, and for each ton of rock raised to the surface, 26 tons of water were pumped to a height of 200ft. One million bolts were used, plus 270,000 tons of concrete and 82,000 tons of cast-iron to line the tunnel walls, and the average cover of rock, gravel and clay between its top and the river is 35ft. A second road tunnel, Kingsway, opened in 1971.

Today Liverpool, of course, is also a centre of great learning. The University of Liverpool is one of the UK's leading universities, renowned for its world-class teaching and research. Six faculties, eight Nobel Laureates to date, 54 departments and schools, nearly 3,000 international students and over 400 industry partners, and a splendid campus to match.

Liverpool John Moores University has an influence stretching far further than the city boundaries. It boasts 20,000 students and 2,500 staff, plus new developments like the Liverpool Science Park on Mount Pleasant, encouraging knowledge-based businesses and nurturing talent in higher education.

Littlewoods founder John Moores

making history

1779
William Roscoe, poet, MP, philanthropist and abolitionist, buys Allerton Hall.

1790
James Maury becomes America's first overseas consul when Washington appoints him to Liverpool. He serves until 1829, residing at No4 Rodney Street.

1802
American Chamber of Commerce opens in Liverpool. Lyceum opens as Europe's first circulating library.

1806
Town's population reaches 80,000.

1807
Abolition of the slave trade in Britain.

1813
Abolition of the East India Company's monopoly of trade with India, aiding Liverpool's trade with the Far East.

making history

1815

First steamboats introduced on the Mersey. First steam ferry boats, to cross the Mersey, arrive two years later.

1830

Opening of the Liverpool-Manchester railway, the world's first passenger locomotive system.

1832

Cholera outbreak in Liverpool kills 1,523 people. Kitty Wilkinson opens her kitchen to sufferers.

1837

First Grand National is run at Aintree (adopts its famous title ten years later). Foundation stone of St George's Hall is laid in 1838.

1842

Liverpool opens the first public baths and washhouses in the country.

1845

Irish Famine brings thousands to Liverpool. Most emigrate to America, but over 80,000 remain. Dr Duncan appointed public medical officer for Liverpool, the first such appointment in the world.

AIR RAIDS THAT SHOOK THE CITY
Honouring those who made the supreme sacrifice...

Merseyside suffered heavily during the Second World War, with whole swathes of the city centre destroyed by air raids. In May 1941 alone, sirens sounded 509 times. The poignant Cenotaph was actually unveiled in 1930 for Liverpool's dead in the First World War. It features two 30ft bronze reliefs – one side with mourners in a cemetery, the other with soldiers marching in rank. The latter's inscription comes from the Book of Ezekiel: 'Out of the north parts...a great company and a mighty army'. A Second World War plaque was added in 1946.

Derby Square, and the Victoria Monument is miraculously unscathed by the Blitz

County Road, Walton

AS·UNKNOWN·AND·YET·WELL·KNOWN·AS·DYING·AND·BEHOLD·WE·LIVE

·OF·THE·NORTH·PARTS···A·GREAT·COMPANY·AND·A·MIGHTY·ARMY

Cenotaph, St George's Plateau

making history

1858
Mersey Docks &
Harbour Board
established.

1860
Central Library &
Museum open on
William Brown
Street.

1874
Everton FC founded
and later become
original members
of Football League.

1876
Walker Art Gallery
opens.

1880
Queen Victoria
grants Liverpool
city status.

1885
The Mersey Railway
Tunnel is completed
after four years.

1892
Liverpool Football
Club founded.

1893
The Overhead
Railway is opened.

1898
First electric trams
run in the city.

1903
Liverpool University
is granted a charter
(it had been estab-
lished in 1881 as
University College).

Lewis's, gutted

Air raid damage on Red Cross Street on 1 January 1941

There's another moving monument to Liverpool's home-based casualties of war at Anfield Cemetery – the May Blitz Memorial unveiled in 1951 that marks a 170ft long communal grave for some 554 victims (373 unidentified) of the most intense period of bombing raids upon Merseyside during the whole of the Second World War. Symbols of faith are absent from the memorial because the grave contains persons of unknown nationality and religion. Further north, Bootle, a strategically-important hub of factories and transportation links throughout the conflict, was also heavily bombed during the infamous May Blitz, with 75 per cent of its dwellings destroyed or damaged and half of its commerce incapacitated.

🏴 LIVERPOOL FIRSTS

The first shot in the American Civil War was fired in 1861 from a gun made by Liverpool firm Fawcett and Preston

Blitz memorial at St Nicholas Church

making history

1904
Foundation stone of the Liverpool Cathedral laid.

1906
Liverpool FC win the Football League, Everton win the FA Cup – an historic double that is to be repeated in 1966 and 1984.

1907
Lusitania makes her maiden voyage from Liverpool. Celebrates its 700th anniversary.

1911
General transport strike in Liverpool. Seamen, dockers, railwaymen and tram drivers strike for better pay and conditions.

FAITH IN A CITY OF EVERY DENOMINATION
From hulking giants to intimate places of worship...

Just over two decades after Pope John Paul II's visit to Liverpool, 2004 was designated as the city's Year of Faith. In the past, churches serving the German, Greek, Italian, Welsh, Polish and Swedish populations were established due to Liverpool's importance as a centre of shipping, and new arrivals have since expanded the diversity of faith. Today the two landmark buildings are the Liverpool and Metropolitan cathedrals. The former was 100 years old in 2004 and, at 101,000sq ft, is the fifth largest cathedral in the world (behind St Peter's in Rome, St John in New York, Nativity of Mary in Milan and Mary of the Chair in Seville). 'Paddy's Wigwam' boasts the world's largest stained-glass window in its Lantern Tower. Together they're linked by Hope Street. But if any thoroughfare epitomises religious diversity, it's Princes Avenue with its fabulous Old Hebrew Congregation Synagogue, exotic Greek Orthodox Church of St Nicholas and imposing Welsh Presbyterian Church.

Pope John Paul II at the Metropolitan Cathedral, 1982

Above: Bishop of Liverpool David Shepphard meets Pope John Paul II in 1982
Left: Princes Road Synagogue
Below: Prayers at Toxteth Mosque

making history

1933
Opening of Speke Airport, the UK's first provincial airport.

1934
Queensway – the longest underwater road tunnel in the world – and the East Lancashire Road opened.

1940
John Lennon is born.

1941
During one week in May, the Luftwaffe drop 2,315 bombs, 119 land mines and countless incendiaries on Merseyside. Almost 4,000 people are killed, 3,500 seriously injured and 70,000 made home-less. Many historic buildings destroyed or badly damaged.

1957
Celebrates its 750th anniversary with special exhibitions, sports tournaments, parades and parties.

1959
Bill Shankly arrives as Liverpool FC's new manager. Things will never quite be the same again.

1961
The Beatles first play at the Cavern Club on Mathew Street.

LIVERPOOL FIRSTS

Completed in 1814, St George's in Everton was the world's first cast-iron church, its parts made at John Cragg's Mersey Iron Foundry

making history

1963
Halewood opens its new Ford car plant.

1977
Liverpool FC win the European Cup as part of an unprecedented 'treble' of silverware. The following year they become the first British side to retain the trophy.

1981
Toxteth Riots. Environment secretary Michael Heseltine spends three weeks in Liverpool. Later recalls: "Alone, every night, I would stand with a glass of wine, looking out at the magnificent view over the river, and ask myself what had gone wrong for this great English city'. Establishes Merseyside Development Corporation. Albert Dock is redeveloped to tune of £20million, and Tate Liverpool opens.

1982
The Boys From The Black Stuff, written by Alan Bleasdale, broadcast by the BBC. The first episode of Phil Redmond's Brookside is broadcast on Channel 4's first night.

BEAT OF A DIFFERENT DRUM
Football, music, fun. Liverpool knows how to have a good time...

Around 150 years after the Slave Trade was abolished came a shipping triangle of an altogether different beat. The rhythms of Africa informed the blues of the Delta. The blues begat rock 'n' roll. And when rock 'n' roll came drifting back down the Mersey... But music had always been there, in the dockland dives and bars. Decades later Cream harnessed the sounds of the street into a superclub of world renown; there was even a typically camp Liverpool take on punk rock, with Eric's club more of a louche European outpost of Warhol's Factory than

any snarling hotbed of anarchy. As for Capital of Culture, just like the football team in Istanbul, the Scousers really wanted it – and they're nobody's fools. Bring the Bolshoi Ballet to the Empire and it'll sell out. Install the SuperLambBanana and it'll be taken to the city's bosom, though no-one can really say why. It just is.

Liverpool FC's homecoming after winning the Champions League in 2005

Everton FC welcomed home after winning the FA Cup in 1966

Young Cilla Black and Gerry Marsden at the Cavern in the 1960s

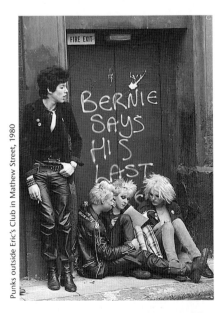
Punks outside Eric's Club in Mathew Street, 1980

making history

1984
International Garden Festival opens in Liverpool, billed as 'a five-month pageant of horticultural excellence and entertainment'.

1989
During FA Cup semi-final at Hillsborough, 96 Liverpool FC fans are killed.

1992
Club Cream starts on Wolstenholme Square.

1996
Liverpool Institute for Performing Arts opens.

2003
Liverpool is chosen as European Capital of Culture for 2008.

2004
City is inscribed as World Heritage Site by UNESCO.

2005
Liverpool FC beat AC Milan in thrilling style to win the Uefa Champions League, their fifth European Cup success.

2006
Over 30 cranes on the skyline, and an estimated £3billion worth of investment in the city.

▶ LIVERPOOL FIRSTS

In 1953 Liverpool-born singer Lita Roza became the first British woman to top the singles charts with How Much is that Doggie in the Window? It's a cover of the Patty Page US hit. Lita's Spanish father played piano in Liverpool clubs

Creamfields in 2006

'Liverpool made more music than most cities, and made it more passionately, because it was in the personality of Liverpool to do so. And Liverpool has the personality it has because it is a seaport. Liverpool only exists because it is a seaport. Its virtues and vices, its accent and attitude, its insularity and its open-mindedness, are all derived from that primary fact'
Paul Du Noyer, Liverpool: Wondrous Place, 2002

'[The Thames] is a wretched river after the Mersey, and the ships are not like the Liverpool ships, and the docks are barren of beauty... But it is a beastly hole after Liverpool; for Liverpool is the town of my heart and I would rather sail a mud-flat there than command a clipper ship out of London'
John Masefield, poet laureate, 1930-67

'My love of New York is something to do with Liverpool. There is the same quality of energy in both cities'
John Lennon, 1971

New Brighton's many faces through the years

The Rialto, Grafton and Locarno are old dancehalls dear to the hearts of a generation of Liverpudlians – all of them, incidentally, played by The Beatles in their formative years. For outdoor fun, there's always been the beaches – Crosby, Formby and Ainsdale to the north, and Wirral's picturesque sands across the Mersey. Also over the water, New Brighton Tower – patterned on the world-famous Eiffel Tower in Paris and completed in 1896. It boasted an assembly hall, winter gardens, refreshment rooms and the all-important ballroom – one of the largest in the world with a dance band stage. Four lifts took sightseers to the top of the structure, from where one could see the Isle of Man, Welsh hills and Lake District.

Left, above and below: ragamuffins on the city streets and the Steble Fountain
Below: Liverpool's black community is arguably the oldest in the country

A MELANGE OF PEOPLES AND CULTURE
Influences from all over the world define Liverpudlians...

The port of Liverpool is one of the most recognisable skylines in the world, and the world's cultural trading routes have embraced it since the 18th Century. The sheer variety of goods, spices, raw materials – and people – that flooded into Liverpool, helped create its character and wealth. The Irish (over one million 'took the ship' to Liverpool between 1845-52), Chinese (the 15m, gold, red and green Chinese Arch is a gift from sister city Shanghai), Caribbean and African diaspora have all added to the mix (the catch-all expression 'la' has its roots in the African/Arabian communities who settled around Liverpool 8 at the turn of the 20th Century).

The landmark Unity development off Chapel Street

L1 development Opposite Albert Dock

LIVERPOOL, A 21ST CENTURY CITY
New developments take shape...

Welcome to a city reborn, exciting and inspiring – and an epicentre for fashion, festivals and, well, having fun. Liverpool looks good for her age, especially from the river. Indeed the waterfront is in the process of being connected by a continuous network of walkways, improved public realm and a canal link. It's the focal point of 120km of coastline between Southport and the Wirral now known as the Mersey Waterfront Regional Park. In Liverpool there'll be a £12million cruise-liner facility in place in 2007, with Cunard proposing to name a new 85,000-ton vessel in the shadow of its former HQ.

LIVERPOOL
1207~2007

OFFICIAL SOUVENIR

Mathew Street Festival, Pier Head

New Liverpool One scheduled to open 2008

quote unquote

'It's stunning the way that the city has been transformed and every time I come back I feel so proud. Our historic buildings – the finest collection of civic buildings in Europe – are being looked after like never before. And there has been so much development – the waterfront, for example, looks wonderful. And all this rubs off on the people'
Peter Sissons, 2003

'Liverpool will become a cultural beacon of the world. Capital of Culture is a wonderful accolade. It is fabulous. You are a wonderful city. I am so glad you won'
Tessa Jowell, culture secretary, 2003

'There is no town in England, London excepted, that can equal Liverpool for the fineness of the streets, the beauty of the buildings; many of the houses are all of stone and the rest (the new part) of brick'
Daniel Defoe,
A Tour Through the Whole Island of Great Britain, 1724

🕊 LIVERPOOL FIRSTS

The world's first scheduled transatlantic passenger service was conducted from 1840 by the wooden paddle-steamer Britannia, owned by the shipping line founded by Samuel Cunard of Halifax, Nova Scotia, and George Burns and David MacIver of Glasgow and Liverpool

ALL-NEW LIVERPOOL TAKES SHAPE
From the waterfront to the city centre, there's a buzz...

Opposite the World Heritage waterfront, the £970million Grosvenor Liverpool One project will put Liverpool back on the map as a shopping destination with the largest city centre regeneration scheme in Europe. Another new jewel of the cultural crown will be the Museum of Liverpool showcasing the city's treasures past, present and future. The new 2.5km canal link, meanwhile, will allow inland boats to sail from the Leeds and Liverpool Canal, past the Pier Head and into the Albert Dock.

It'll include two new locks, five new bridges and a tunnel, with seating close to the water and shelter from the wind. Further south, a world-class development at King's Dock has been designed by architects Wilkinson & Eyre, with lots of street furniture, cafés and parks around a £146million Arena & Conference Centre and riverside walkway to the Albert Dock. The masterplan envisages 'a mixed-use waterfront quarter containing high-quality apartments, prestige hotels, and leisure and retail facilities'.

To the north and just past the Pier Head, Prince's Dock is at the hub of the waterfront renaissance and home to luxury apartments, the Crowne Plaza and Malmaison Hotels and private bankers Coutts. For a century it was a conduit of world history – the departure point for nine million emigrants sailing to America from 1821 onwards. Who knows how many famous names in today's USA have ancestors that walked down its gangways?

King's Dock Arena

quote unquote

'This commercial intercourse of the inhabitants, induces a general harmony and sociability, unclouded by those ceremonies and distinctions that are met with in more polished life; hence the freedom and animation which the town has always been observed to possess'
Moss, Liverpool Guide 1796

'I have never seen any place like Liverpool. Liverpudlians are proud of their birth place, not only for its history, supremacy as a sea port, delightful situation and surroundings, but because of its pre-eminence of its merchant princes and citizens stability, integrity and humour'
Recollections of a Liverpudlian, 1908

'Liverpool Cathedral is one of the great buildings of the world. Suddenly one realises that the greatest art of architecture, that compels reverence, but also lifts one up, and turns one into a king, is the art of enclosing space'
John Betjeman, poet laureate, 1970

Street festivals and fashion shows

♥ LIVERPOOL FIRSTS

In 1960, venerable Liverpool institution Martins Bank became the first bank in the world to use a computer

800 REASONS TO CELEBRATE

JANUARY 2007

Monday 1 January: 160th anniversary of Dr William Henry Duncan appointed world's first medical officer of health;
Monday 1 January: 150th anniversary of the Mersey Docks and Harbour Board

Liverpool Reads
'Small Island' by Andrea Levy

The 2007 Liverpool Reads initiative will forge links with Bristol, Hull and Glasgow, exploring themes of ethnicity, nationality and love and offers specific links to slavery remembrance projects.

50th Anniversary
Cavern Concerts
Cavern City Tours
The Cavern, Mathew Street
Tuesday 16 to Sunday 21 January

The Roscoe Lectures
Liverpool John Moores University
St George's Hall
Wednesday 17 January

Trevor Philips – Understanding the Lessons of the Killing of Anthony Walker.

Liverpool Echoes
Royal Liverpool Philharmonic Orchestra
Philharmonic Hall
First concert: Thursday 18 January 7.30pm

Liverpool's 800th birthday is the inspiration for six concerts celebrating artists, music and musical events connected with the Phil and the musical history of the city.

Anthony Brown's 100
Heads Thinking as One
Liverpool, Its History,
Its Places, Its People
Wednesday 24 January to Saturday 10 February: The Capital Building, Old Hall Street.
On tour until October

A truly unique and fascinating exhibition of mixed media portraits by Liverpool artist Anthony Brown. Revealing 100 subjects chosen for their unique contribution to Liverpool life and the 'Charter Canvas' which features Merseyside's ancestry.

The Cathedral That Never Was
National Museums Liverpool
Walker Art Gallery
Saturday 27 January
to Sunday 22 April

Following a programme of major conservation work at Liverpool's National Conservation Centre, the stunning architect's model of Lutyens' cathedral brings to life the story of an amazing and ambitious building proposed for Liverpool.

FEBRUARY 2007

Thursday 22 February: Birkenhead forms world's first scout group 100 years ago

Black Audio Film Collective
FACT, Wood Street
February to March

City Charters Exhibition
Picton Reading Room,
Liverpool Central Library
February to June. Free

Liverpool's most important documents from charters and maps to banknotes and photographs go on show.

The Roscoe Lectures
Liverpool John Moores University
St George's Hall
Thursday 8 February: Professor John Barrow – Our Place in the Universe

Wednesday 28 February: Lord Goldsmith, QC Attorney General – How Law Holds Together a Civil Society.

The Elements
The Pool of Life
The Royal Court Theatre
Wednesday 14 February 8.00pm

The first major international collaboration between Chinese and UK artists.

Chinese New Year
Nelson St and Berry Street
Sunday 18 February. Free

Chinese New Year graces the oldest Chinese community in Europe. 2007 is Year of the Pig.

Centre of the Creative Universe:
Liverpool and the Avant-Garde
Tate Liverpool, Albert Dock
Tuesday 20 February
to Saturday 9 September

Major exhibition explores how artists contributed to an external view of Liverpool over the past four decades.

Reflections on Faith,
History and Culture
Our Lady and St Nicholas,
Liverpool Parish Church
Wednesday 21 February
to Friday 30 March 1.05pm

Continuing a century-old Lent tradition of daily talks featuring bishops, politicians and special guests.

Around the Pool in 800 Years
St George's Hall
Tuesday 22, Thursday 23 and Saturday 24 February

Second-year students from Liverpool John Moores University's Drama Department proudly present a new piece of theatre for the 2007 birthday.

WONDROUS PLACES

In 2004 the national launch of English Heritage Open Days was held, appropriately enough, in the country's latest World Heritage Site – more specifically St George's Hall where the Small Concert Room was opened for the first time in over 20 years.

In 2007, there will be a specially extended, month-long Heritage Open Days season (29 August to 21 September) to give the people of Liverpool even more chance to celebrate their city's fantastic architecture, culture and heritage. Local property openings and events will be organised by the Civic Trust, Liverpool Culture Company, civic societies, museums, and owners and managers of buildings.

Among the gems on show in recent years: no16 Cook Street, designed by Peter Ellis in 1866, with its modernist glass frontage and beautiful cast-iron staircase inside; the Oratory, John Foster's Greek Revival temple near the Liverpool Cathedral dating from 1827; Liverpool Medical Institution, built on Mount Pleasant in 1836 and boasting a fabulous floor mosaic and historic library; County Sessions House on William Brown Street, from 1884 and a wonderfully complex building with Renaissance decorative detail; and the Athenaeum on Church Alley, 210 years old and predating both its namesake in London and the Garrick Club. And that's just for starters.

MARCH 2007

Thursday 1 March: 170th Anniversary of first Grand National;
Sunday 25 March: 200th Anniversary of the Abolition of the British Slave Trade.

LEAP Dance Festival
Merseyside Dance Initiative
Various Venues
1 to 10 March

Celebrating its 15th year featuring Russell Maliphant, Serge-Aime Coulibaly and Maresa Von Stockert.

Mendelssohn's ELIJAH
Liverpool Welsh Choral
Philharmonic Hall
Sunday 4 March 7.30pm

Liverpool Performing Arts Festival
Liverpool Culture Company
St George's Hall
5 to 9 March and 19 to 23 March

Liverpool's St George's Hall will come alive to the sound of more than 7,000 performers participating in the Liverpool Performing Arts Festival.

Royal Liverpool Philharmonic Orchestra
Stephen Hough Residency
Philharmonic Hall
Thursday 8 March 7.30pm
Sunday 11 March 2.30pm
Saturday 17 March 7.30pm

Wirral History and Heritage Fair
Wirral Museum.
Saturday 10 March

Displays and talks by Wirral's Heritage and History group.

The Roscoe Lectures
Liverpool John Moores University
St George's Hall
Monday 12 March

Esther Rantzen –
The Protection Society needs to provide to prevent Vulnerable Children from Exploitation and Abuse.

Thursday 22 March
Peter Sutherland KCMG (venue tbc) – Citizenship, Globalisation, Free Trade & Fair Trade – the Role of Multi Nationals.

Ecumenical Service of Penitence
Slavery Remembrance
Liverpool Anglican Cathedral
Saturday 24 March 11.30am

Public Debate
National Museums Liverpool
Sunday 25 March

Public debate focussing on contemporary black issues.

John Newton Promenade
Liverpool Culture Company
Albert Dock
Sunday 25 March

Performance featuring the story of slavery in Liverpool ending with a rousing chorus of Newton's hymn, Amazing Grace.

Contemporary Art from China
Tate Liverpool, Albert Dock
Friday 30 March to Sunday 10 June

Liverpool has always embraced its thriving Chinese community and this is reflected in this illuminating exhibition.

HALL OF PLENTY

Welcome to the royal favourite. On a tour of Liverpool in 1851, Queen Victoria said St George's Hall was "worthy of ancient Athens, the architecture is so simple and magnificent." More recently Prince Charles called it "one of the greatest public buildings of the last 200 years which sits in the centre of one of Europe's finest cities." And on 23 April, a day-long series of celebrations will mark the completion of its £23million refurbishment. The highlights will be the re-opening of the Small Concert Room – in operation for the first time since World War II – and the opening of a new Visitor Centre.

This 490ft long, neo-classical masterpiece was designed by 25-year-old Harvey Lonsdale Elmes. In 1858 Charles Dickens staged the first of several public readings in Liverpool here – an event recreated in December 2006 with the 'Penny Readings' organised by the University of Liverpool's Reader magazine. The Great Hall's 7,737-pipe organ is the third largest in the UK (after London's Albert Hall and the Liverpool Cathedral), and the exquisite, once-covered sunken floor of blue and brown Minton tiles will be revealed for viewing for the re-opening. On the six pairs of bronze doors inside are the letters SPQL, an adaptation of the motto of Rome and meaning 'to the Senate and the People of Liverpool'. Outside, a pride of four lions, each 14ft long, stand guard.

In August, it'll stage 100 Heads Thinking as One, a touring exhibition of mixed media portraits in celebration of Liverpool's here, now and future, by artist Tony Brown. All 100 subjects have been chosen for their unique contribution to Liverpool life. Some have achieved celebrity, others have achieved success in their chosen field, but all have achieved 'a magnitude of spirit and passion for their city'. From 14-16 September, meanwhile, St George's Hall hosts The Big History Show – 800 Years of Liverpool.

This three-day local history fair, organised in partnership with BBC Radio Merseyside and University of Liverpool, will be in the Great Hall to showcase Liverpool's history and the work of its historical societies. The Small Concert Room will host a conference – entitled Liverpool: a sense of time and place – at which leading academics examine the competing and contested images and representations of the city.

APRIL 2007

160th anniversary of the opening of Birkenhead Park which was used as a template for New York's Central Park

Coming of Age
Liverpool Culture Company
Across the city
April to May

Liverpool school children will celebrate their generation and their place within Liverpool culture. 22 projects to be devised in collaboration with 22 arts organisations.

The Lord Made These
Blessings For Us
Liverpool Metropolitan Cathedral
of Christ the King
April to September

This exhibition features displays, artefacts and information on aspects of Liverpool's 800-year heritage based upon the motto: 'The Lord made these blessings for us'.

The Grand National
Aintree Race Course
Thursday 12 to Saturday 14 April

The world's most famous steeple chase, races into its 170th year.

The Water's Edge: Women's Work
and the Liverpool Waterfront
Open Eye Gallery
Friday 13 April to Saturday 2 June

Michelle Sank photographs 30 women who work, or have worked, on the Liverpool waterfront. Also includes an oral history project with 50 people whose stories span the period from WWII to the present day.

Seafarers and Emigrants Exhibition
The Swedish Seaman's Church and
the Liverpool International Nordic
Community Scandinavian Seaman's
Church
Sunday 22 April to Sunday 20 May

Gala re-opening of St George's Hall
Liverpool Culture Company
and National Museums Liverpool,
St George's Hall
Monday 23 April: St George's Day.

A day long series of celebrations will mark the completion of the £23m refurbishment of one of the world's finest examples of neo-classical architecture. The highlights will be the re-opening of the stunning Small Concert Room, the opening of a new Visitor Centre displaying the Singh Twins' special commission and a city-wide Bell Symphony.

Sudley House reopens
National Museums Liverpool
Sudley House
Spring 2007

Sudley House, the former family home of the Liverpool merchant George Holt, has been undergoing a crucial redevelopment and will reopen. The house will be transformed with new displays, improved access and a temporary exhibition space.

MAY 2007

Wednesday 30 May: 25th anniversary of Pope John Paul II visit to Liverpool; Friday 25 May: 30th anniversary of Liverpool FC's first European Cup win

A1 & A1
FACT, Wood Street
May to July

From the Archbishop of Liverpool, Patrick Kelly to Steven Gerrard, this film incorporates people into simulated spaces and landscapes inspired by the city and its history.

Four Corners
Liverpool Culture Company
Across the city
May

All five neighbourhoods in the city will work with an arts organisation to develop programmes around identity, climaxing with a series of performances.

Elgar's 150th Birthday Celebrations
Royal Liverpool Philharmonic Orchestra
Vernon Handley CBE conductor
Liverpool Cathedral
12, 16, 17, 24 and 26 May 7.30pm

Halton Literature Festival
Monday 14 to Sunday 20 May

In addition to various performances there will be a host of workshops and classes for all ages and abilities including Writing Your Life Story, Scriptwriting and Writing for Radio Journalism.

Writing on the Wall
2007 Literature Festival
Across the city
Monday 14 to Sunday 20 May

Internationally acclaimed authors, campaigners and renowned social commentators explore the themes of the bicentenary of the abolition of the British slave trade and Liverpool's 800th birthday. Guests include Benjamin Zephaniah, Jean 'Binta' Breeze, Levi Tafari, Ray Costello and Kevin Sampson.

The Trial of James Maybrick
Liverpool Cricket Club, Aigburth
Saturday 19 and Sunday 20 May

Conference on the life and death of Liverpool cotton merchant, Liverpool Cricket Club member and Jack the Ripper suspect James Maybrick, who was allegedly murdered by his wife Florence – whose infamous trial attracted world wide interest. Event highlight of Liverpool Cricket Club's 200th anniversary celebrations in 2007.

Southport International Jazz Festival
Southport
Thursday 31 May to Sunday 3 June

Sample some of the finest jazz, blues and soul in the North West.

JUNE 2007

165th anniversary of opening of world's first public baths and wash houses on Frederick Street by Kitty Wilkinson 1842

Historical Re-enactments
West Derby Village
June

Using the existing buildings of the village as backdrop, this cross generational event will provide the community with an opportunity to take part in re-enactments whilst at the same time learn about the local history of West Derby Village.

Wall Talks
Liverpool Heritage Market Site
June

Producer and director Jen Heyes, screen and stage writer Andrew Sherlock, RSC musician and composer Edward Watson and a fine Liverpool cast bring you this once-in-a-lifetime experience that 'lets the ghosts speak and tell us what they know...' You will never see Liverpool in quite the same way again.

Heritage Sports Day
Liverpool Community Games
Croxteth Hall & Country Park
Sunday 10 June 12:00 to 5:00pm

Display of traditional sports in full period costume. Free.

Bowring Park Centenary
Knowsley
Saturday 9 to Tuesday 12 June

A weekend of fun activities celebrating the centenary of this historic Merseyside Park. Events include a fantastic steam train excursion from Liverpool.

Africa Oyé
Sefton Park
Tuesday 12 to Sunday 17 June

A celebration of heritage and culture from the Caribbean, Brazil, the United States and continental Africa. The main event is in Sefton Park on Saturday and Sunday June 16 and 17. Saturday will celebrate Liverpool's past, present and future through reggae to hip hop and gospel to rumba. Sunday is Africa at its best. Free entry. Visit: africaoye.com

Maritime Festival
Liverpool Culture Company
South and Central Docks
Saturday 16 and Sunday 17 June.
Free.

The River Mersey will host a festival of tall ships and naval vessels.

Sir Paul McCartney's Liverpool Oratorio
Carl Davis CBE conductor
Royal Liverpool Philharmonic Orchestra and Choir with Liverpool Cathedral Choristers Liverpool Cathedral
Saturday 16 June

Celebration of Sir Paul McCartney's 65th Birthday Party
The Cavern, Mathew Street
Monday 18 June

Liverpool's Cunard Yanks
Souled Out Films Philharmonic Hall
Thursday 21 June

World premiere. This fascinating documentary reveals the major impact of Liverpool's Merchant Seamen in the 1950s on the development of Liverpool culture, particularly fashion and music, which laid the foundations for Merseybeat, and of course, The Beatles.

North West Historic Motor Show and Family Extravaganza
Southport
Saturday 23 and Sunday 24 June

Featuring hundreds of historic and modern motor vehicles.

Birkenhead Park Celebrations
Friday 29 June to Sunday 1 July

A weekend celebrating the restoration of Birkenhead Park.

Peter Blake
Tate Liverpool, Albert Dock
Friday 29 June to
Sunday 23 September

Tate Liverpool will present a major retrospective exhibition of paintings by Peter Blake, the largest since his Tate Gallery exhibition in 1983. A highly influential and original artist, Blake is often described as the 'Godfather of British Pop Art'.

REMEMBERING THE SLAVE TRADE

The new International Slavery Museum (ISM) opens its galleries on 23 August, Slavery Remembrance Day. David Fleming, director of National Museums Liverpool, says: "In 1994, NML opened the Transatlantic Slavery Gallery, the first of its kind in the world. Now our vision is to create a major new museum to promote the understanding of transatlantic slavery and its enduring impact."

Also planned...
➤ Liverpool Reads: Small Islands (various venues) January onwards. Collaboration between four partner cities with links to the slave trade.
➤ Black Audio Film Collective (FACT) February-March. Engage with a rich body of film, video and archival material.
➤ Haiti Freedom Sculpture (Maritime Museum) February. Will go on a national tour with its final destination at the ISM.
➤ LEAP Dance Festival (various venues) March. African dance companies invited to perform.
➤ Ecumenical Service of Penitence (Liverpool Cathedral) 24 March.
➤ Public debate (Maritime Museum) 25 March.
➤ Writing on the Wall Festival (various venues) 14-20 May. Special guests include Benjamin Zephaniah, Jean 'Binta' Breeze and Levi Tafari.
➤ Brouhaha International Festival

(city/Princes Park) July. The 2007 theme is 'New Beginnings', year three of the 'Crossing Waters' carnival trilogy.
➤ Interfaith service (St Nicholas Parish Church) 23 August.
➤ Slavery Remembrance Day Community Event (Otterspool Prom) 23 August. Food, speakers, activities and an exhibition of artefacts.
➤ Bound (Open Eye Gallery) August-October. Exploring human enslavement.
➤ Conference on Slavery in the Iberian Atlantic (Maritime Museum) September. Co-ordinated by the School of History at the University of Liverpool.
➤ Black & Asian Studies Association Conference (Maritime Museum) October. History of black peoples in Britain.

JULY 2007

Friday 6 July: 50th anniversary of John Lennon meeting Paul McCartney; Sunday 15 July: 100th anniversary of Opening of Port of Liverpool Building

Cross Artform – Slavery:
Slavery in the 21st Century
Hope Street Ltd
Venue tbc
July

Acclaimed director Hilary Westlake will be creating a multi-media piece focusing on slavery, its abolition in Britain and of slavery in the 21st Century.

Brouhaha International Festival
Brouhaha
July

Celebrating a new three-year carnival arts programme.
Visit: brouhaha.uk.com

Liverpool Arabic Arts Festival 2007
Across the city
First two weeks of July

A lively mixture of cultural activities from the Arabic world and Britain. Dance, music, clubs, visual art, film, architecture, family events and food.

Origins – Early Music Festival
Sunday 1 July to Sunday 8 July

A series of concerts performed in some of Wirral's architectural jewels by early music ensembles featuring Bach, Gabrieli, Vivaldi, Scarlatti, Taverner and Purcell.

Schools Birthday Party
Friday 6 July

Every school in the city will be celebrating Liverpool's 800th birthday. Schools will be supplied party packs with a special commemorative souvenir for pupils.

St.Helens Arts Festival
Saturday 7 to Saturday 14 July

This year's arts festival is based on motion, transport and heritage.

HUB Festival
Liverpool Culture Company
Otterspool Park
Saturday 14 and Sunday15 July. Free

Urban street culture festival celebrating the best of skateboarding, BMX, live music, hip-hop, break-dancing as well as displaying some wicked street art from the professionals.

Children's Boredom Busters
The National Trust
Speke Hall
19, 21, 26 and 28 July and 2, 4, 9 and 11 August

Activities for children focusing on various Tudor and Victorian pastimes to reflect key historical periods in the history of Speke Hall. Includes traditional games, painting, writing and period costumes.

Theatre in the Park
Stadt Moers Park, Whiston
Saturday 21 July to Sunday 22 July

An amazing theatrical journey through Stadt Moers Park, as it becomes a giant promenade theatre venue. Performances also take place at Otterspool Park, Liverpool on 14 and 15 July.

Do You Remember When?
The World of Glass Exhibition
St Helens
Tuesday 24 July to Sunday 2 September

An exhibition of 150 years of St Helens seen through the different decades, giving an overview of each decade, its style and important events.

St. Helens Show
Sherdley Park
Saturday 28 and Sunday 29 July
A fun-filled family event.

A Magical History Tour
Merseyside Maritime Museum
(In collaboration with the
Liverpool Culture Company)
Saturday 28 July 2007
to December 2008

A major exhibition celebrating the
city's 800th birthday in style with a
look back across Liverpool's history.
Told through the lives of its people,
this tour demonstrates ways in which
Liverpool has changed and evolved
over the past eight centuries, from a
tiny fishing village to a Victorian
metropolis of global significance.
Iconic objects on display include the
Liverpool charters and a
reconstruction of the long-lost
Liverpool Castle. Free entry.

AUGUST 2007

*Tuesday 28 August: 800th anniversary of
King John granting Liverpool's first
charter*

Celebration of Leeds Liverpool Canal
Hope Street Ltd Canal side
August
Multi-award-winning artist John
Fox directs a production employing
professional artists and a broad
range of community groups that will
culminate in performances
celebrating Liverpool and Leeds'
800th birthdays. The piece will be
performed in, alongside, on and
above the Leeds Liverpool canal.

Poetry In The City (PiC)
Across the city
August
Poetry In The City will be hosting
a series of events based around the
themes of slavery and liberation in
all their manifestations.

B O U N D
Open Eye Gallery
Friday 10 August to
Saturday20 October
International artists represent
personal perspectives on the physical
and psychological impact of slavery
on humanity, through photography,
video, live art performance,
interventions and installations.

Tudor Life Weekend
The National Trust
Speke Hall
Saturday 4 - Sunday 5 August
16th Century life at Speke Hall is
recreated through Tudor music, food
and drink; various Tudor pastimes,
children's traditional activities and
period costumed interpretation.

Woodvale Rally
Formby By-Pass
Saturday 4 and Sunday 5 August
Hugely popular heritage automobile
and air show.

Medieval Mersey Traders
Norton Priory Museum
& Gardens, Runcorn
Saturday 4 and Sunday 5 August
A 15th Century living history
encampment demonstrating crafts
and skills used at Norton Priory.

Knowsley Flower Show
Court Hey Park
Sunday 5 August 11.00am to 5.00pm
Affiliated to the Royal Horticultural
Society, the show offers budding
gardeners and novices the
opportunity to enter more than
100 classes.

B O U N D
Open Eye Gallery
Friday 10 August to
Saturday 20 October
International artists represent
personal perspectives on the physical
and psychological impact of slavery
on humanity, through photography,
video, live art performance,
interventions and installations.

Southport Flower Show
Victoria Park
Thursday 16 to Sunday 19 August
Now in its 78th year, the 2007
event is on course to attract
record breaking 80,000 visitors.

Memorial Lecture:
Slavery Remembrance
August 22 tbc

International Day for
the Commemoration
of Slavery and its Abolition
UNESCO
Thursday 23 August
Liverpool has hosted a Slavery
Remembrance Day event since
1999 in recognition of the city's
role in the Transatlantic Slave Trade.

Events include:
➤ Interfaith Service
Liverpool Community Spirit,
St. Nicholas Parish Church
➤ Libation Service
Liverpool Waterfront
Traditional African ceremony,
commemorates the lives and
deaths of slaves.
➤ International Slavery
Museum Opening
Merseyside Maritime Museum
The city's major new £10m museum is
to open on 23 August 2007 to mark
the 200th-year anniversary of the
abolition of the slave trade in Britain.

Mathew Street Music Festival
Liverpool Culture Company
Liverpool City Centre
Friday 24 to Monday 27 August
Europe's biggest FREE city centre music
festival is going retro for 2007 in
celebration of Liverpool's 800 years!

Liverpool 800 Day
City-wide celebrations
Tuesday 28 August
A dazzling civic and community
procession, a thanksgiving service, a
host of community parties and what
is set to be the largest firework display
Europe has ever seen will mark the
800th anniversary of the granting of
Liverpool's first Charter by King John
in 1207.

Heritage Open Days
Across the region
Wednesday 29 August to
Friday 21 September
A specially extended month-long
season will give people even more
chance to celebrate our fantastic
architecture, culture and heritage.
Local property openings and events
will be organised by the Civic Trust,
Liverpool Culture Company, civic
societies, museums, and owners and
managers of buildings.

Liverpool's 800th Birthday Concert
Empire Theatre
Wednesday 30 August

SEPTEMBER 2007

Friday 7 September: 100th anniversary of maiden voyage of Lusitania from Liverpool-New York

Sugar
Liverpool-Marseille
Dance Collaboration
Liverpool
September

Live urban dance performances in Liverpool's public spaces.

Extraordinary Journey
Royal Liverpool Hospital,
School of Tropical Medicine,
Women's Hospital
September - December

This multi-media health festival celebrates past successes and advances in all health and social care using the creative arts. The festival will be launched at The Big History Show with events to take place in various health settings including Liverpool Royal Hospital.

Welsh Roots/Routes
Eloquent Suitcase Exhibition
Friday 7 to Sunday 16 September - 08 Place
Tuesday 18 to Monday 24 September - Liverpool Cathedral
Tuesday 25 to Sunday 30 September Alima Centre 35 Sefton Street

The Welsh Routes project is an exploration and celebration of the Welsh heritage in Liverpool.

Honda Formula4-Stroke
Powerboat Series
Liverpool Waterfront
September. Free

Cycle Tour of Great Britain
Liverpool Presents
Sefton Park
Friday 14 September. Free

Liverpool hosts the start of the North West stage of the nation's premier cycling event.

Clipper Round-the-World
Yacht Race Start (07-08)
Albert Dock
Saturday 15 September. Free

The Big History Show
- 800 Years of Liverpool
St George's Hall
Friday 14 to Sunday 16 September

A three-day local history fair, organised by the Liverpool Culture Company in partnership with BBC Radio Merseyside, National Museums Liverpool and the Liverpool universities, will be in the Great Hall to showcase Liverpool's history and the work of its historical societies. The Small Concert room will host a conference - entitled 'Liverpool: a sense of time and place' - at which leading academics examine the competing and contested images and representations of the city.

River Mersey Cruise Liner Facility
Official Opening
Friday 21 September

The QE2 returns to Liverpool on its 40th anniversary cruise to open the city's new £15m cruise facility.

Southport Airshow
and Military Display
Southport Seafront
Saturday 22 and
Sunday 23 September

Combining a spectacular air display with a host of ground attractions featuring Red Arrows, RAF jets, World War II bombers and helicopters, skydivers performing death-defying displays along the seafront.

Vintage Fair Organ
and Steam Rally
Victoria Park, Widnes
Saturday 29 September

TATE LIVERPOOL

For the first time in its 24-year history, the Turner Prize is taking place outside London – and Tate Liverpool is the venue. The 2007 show will be a curtain-raiser for Capital of Culture, with the exhibition of four short-listed artists running from 19 October to 13 January 2008. Christoph Grunenberg, director of Tate Liverpool, will be chairing a jury of national and international calibre. "The Turner Prize will bring a welcome focus to the city and generate thought-provoking discussion around contemporary art." The shortlisted artists will be revealed on 8 May and the winner announced on 3 December.

Centre of the Creative Universe: Liverpool and the Avant-Garde runs at Tate Liverpool from 20 Feb to 9 Sept. To coincide with the 800th celebrations, this major exhibition investigates how the city has inspired a diverse range of important post-war artists. It takes its title from a statement by Allen Ginsberg, explores how artists have contributed to an external view of Liverpool in people's imaginations, and reveals – as well as challenges – myths of the city's creative scene over the past four decades. In that time Liverpool has emerged as a centre of global pop culture, a source of inspiration for documentary photography and politically-motivated tendencies, and played host to a series of major avant-garde artists and movements.

OCTOBER 2007

120th anniversary of Britain's first Mosque (Brougham Terrace)

Cultiv8 and Cultural Awakening Festival
October

A Three-day festival of African and Caribbean dance and Cultiv8, a seminar to discuss African and Caribbean arts in the UK.

Bluecoat Reopens
Autumn

After a £10m refurbishment, the city centre's oldest building and the UK's oldest arts centre, re-opens with a superb new wing, housing galleries and a performance space designed by international architects BIQ from Rotterdam.

Black History Month
Across the region
October

A wide and lively range of performances, exhibitions, talks and gatherings which acknowledge the long presence and contribution to Liverpool of people of African descent.

Cains Liverpool Irish Festival
Across the city
October

More than 50 events will take place at venues across the city, spanning folk, contemporary and rock music, theatre, poetry, lectures, films and nightclubs.

British Musical Fireworks Championships
Southport
Friday 5 to Sunday 7 October

Britain's leading pyrotechnic companies compete in the ultimate fireworks battle.

Heritage Twilight Tours
Speke Hall
Saturday 6 & 13 October and Saturday 10 November

Enjoy exclusive 'after hours' tours of Speke Hall in its atmospheric twilight setting. A costumed guide will take you through the hall's rooms and corridors, explaining the beliefs and superstitions of some of this 16th century building's former residents. Costumed musicians will serenade you with Tudor music on your tour.

The Sacrifice
James MacMillan
Welsh National Opera and Liverpool Culture Company
Thursday 16 October 7:15pm

English premiere. A story of love, revenge and reconciliation, inspired by the heightened mythical world of The Mabinogion, a collection of ancient Welsh folktales. Tickets from £10 to £37 - check wno.org.uk and liverpool08.com for details of special pricing promotions. Composed and conducted by one of the world's greatest living composers, James MacMillan, The Sacrifice is directed by Katie Mitchell with a libretto by the poet Michael Symmons Roberts.

Turner Prize
Tate Liverpool, Albert Dock
Friday 19 October 2007
to Sunday 13 January 2008

The UK's most prestigious annual art competition will be held outside London for the first time since it began in 1984.

The Jamaican Big Draw
Speke Hall
October (half-term)

A chance to paint and draw art inspired by the West Indies in commemoration of the 200th-year anniversary of the abolition of the slave trade in Britain.

Liverpool Lantern Parade
Sefton Park
Wednesday 31 October. Free

The Liverpool Lantern Company stages its brilliant Halloween Day of the Dead parade in Sefton Park as the community lights up the dark with lanterns and illuminated structures beautifully designed.

CREATIVE COMMUNITIES

A ground-breaking community programme in Liverpool unlocks the potential of tens of thousands of people from all walks of life. An experienced team of more than 12 people help bring the ideas into reality plus more than 100 projects are funded by grants annually to help people realise their creative dreams.

An arts project in the Four Corners of the city, a major play based on the memories of black and minority ethnic merchant seamen (Cruel Sea) and a musical talent contest for young people (Streetwaves) are just some of the exciting projects. Theatre will enliven the parks, sport will be brought to the neighbourhoods in a massive community games, plus wide-ranging schools projects all make sure that 2007 will be a year to remember.

Projects include:

➤ Merseyside Association of Ghanaians: hospital and home-visiting programme; Merseyside-Ghana school link

➤ Rotunda Community College: a theatrical production through the eyes of the young in the north inner-city area

➤ Come Alive @ 55: tapestry depicting history of Speke Garston run by older people

➤ Eric Lynch: series of one-man interactive performances to do with the slave trade.

➤ Jah Jussa: documentary telling the story of city engineer John Alexander Brodie who invented the football goal net in the 1890s.

➤ Mel Stapleford: Kaleidoscope Heritage Project, encouraging over-55s in sheltered accommodation to reminisce.

➤ Merseyside Archaeological Society: Will advance knowledge of archaeology across Merseyside.

➤ Stanley House Academy: Young people will investigate football history in L8.

Parades and pageants will bring the streets of the city to life, a Children's festival will provide excitement for young people in their summer holiday and 22 schools projects will form the programme Coming of Age where young people celebrate their place within the generations of Liverpool.

People in all neighbourhoods will be touched by projects of all sizes, including a mass-participation project called Liverpool Reads, a secondary school violence awareness programme and more festivals than you can imagine, run by local people, for local people. The message is: Get out there and get involved!

NOVEMBER 2007

Thursday 22 November: 210th anniversary of founding of Athenaeum - UK's oldest gentlemen's club

Homotopia 2007
Across the city
November

Liverpool's annual celebration of lesbian and gay art and culture. 2007 sees the festival grow to new heights with three weeks of quality theatre, film, talks, human rights debates, heritage, art, video, music and club nights. This year Homotopia will commission four new plays by established and emerging gay writers.

DaDaFest
Liverpool
November

The largest celebration of Disability and Deaf art in the UK, bringing together internationally acclaimed professional artists, home grown talent and up and coming young artists.

Nick Crowe and Ian Rawlinson
FACT, Wood St
November 2007 to January 2008

See off 2007 and welcome 2008 with a bang. The main exhibition space at FACT will be alight with Roman candles, Catherine Wheels and

Chinese Crackers all set off to a precise firing schedule and the display will be filmed.

November 5th Fireworks
City parks
Monday 5 November. Free

Liverpool celebrates the anniversary of Guy Fawkes. Tens of thousands of people are expected to witness the displays which will be synchronised to music.

International Guitar Festival of Great Britain
Various venues
Friday 9 to Sunday 25 November

Wirral's 19th International Guitar Festival presents a stunning programme of concerts performed by top-flight performers from across the globe. www.bestguitarfest.com

Liverpool Music Week
Liverpool
November 17 to November 25

Christmas Lights Switch-On
St George's Hall Plateau
Friday 18 November. Free

A spectacular show marks the start of the festive season and the whole family is guaranteed a magical atmosphere and an evening of fabulous, festive fun.

Family and Familiar Trees
Liverpool Culture Company
Across the city
Wednesday 21 November to Wednesday 5 December

Families across the city will be invited to work with local artists to create portraits of themselves, their family and their favourite trees - celebrating the city's lungs through photography, sculpture, art installations, tree planting and decoration.

The Cornerstone Festival
Cornerstone Building, Hope University
Provisional dates: Friday 23 November to Saturday 8 December

NATIONAL TREASURES

National Museums Liverpool have a scintillating array of exhibitions for 2007. January brings Doves and Dreams: the Art of Frances Macdonald and J Herbert McNair, to the Walker (until 22 April). Alongside Charles Rennie Mackintosh and Margaret Macdonald, the married couple formed the Glasgow Four at the turn of the 20th Century. This exhibition celebrates their considerable yet lesser-known contribution, and the first exploration of their ten years in Liverpool.

Also at the Walker, the original model of Sir Edwin Lutyens' Liverpool Roman Catholic Cathedral, until April. It would've been vast – twice the height of St Paul's in London. Work started in 1933, but only the crypt was completed before post-war austerity stopped work and instead, the Metropolitan Cathedral of Christ the King was opened in 1967. And at the Walker from 17 November to 24 February 2008, Joseph Wright of Derby showcases the major works of one of the most significant British artists

of the mid-18th Century. The exhibition will focus on the period 1768-1771 when Wright worked in Liverpool. Over at the Lady Lever, the lost interiors of the region's Victorian houses are being shown in a photographic exhibition entitled Merchant Palaces (16 February to 13 May). The Magical History Tour at the Merseyside Maritime Museum (20 July to December) documents 800 years of Liverpool history. Stories will be told through the lives of ordinary people, the famous and infamous. It will explore how different parts of the cityscape have changed and evolved, and how the population of the city has grown and diversified. The exhibition will also look forward to the Liverpool of the future, reflecting aspirations and ambitions for the city in the 21st Century and beyond.

WALKS, TOURS AND CRUISES

➤**Yellow Duckmarine** (0151 708 7799) Hour-long land-and-river tour of waterfront, city and docks, on authentic WWII landing craft ➤**City Sightseeing Tour** (0151 933 2324) Hour-long open-top bus trip of city centre with Blue Badge guide ➤**Mersey Ferries River Explorer Cruise** (0151 630 1030) 50-minute cruise on the Mersey for the best views of Liverpool's spectacular waterfront ➤**Central Library Tour** (0151 233 5844) Fine book collections and historic rooms revealed to the public, second Tuesday of each month ➤**Liverpool Heritage Cab City Tours** (0151 531 6947) Experience the city's history in a taxi or 1920s-style car-hire tour ➤**Radio City Tower** (0151 709 3285) Guided tours around one of the city's most unusual buildings, and unbeatable views ➤**Joseph Williamson Tunnels** (0151 709 6868) Fascinating underground network of tunnels, built in the 19th Century, plus exhibitions depicting the life and times of the eccentric who built them.

➤**Cains Brewery** (0151 709 8734) Victorian brewery producing award-winning tours including buffet and two pints in Brewery Tap pub ➤**City Walks** (0151 652 3692) Explore the city's architecture and art on foot with a Blue Badge guide ➤**Slavery History Trail** (0151 726 0941) Guided tours of areas connected to Liverpool's slave trade ➤**Magical Mystery Tour** (0151 709 3285) Starts at the Beatles Story and ends at Cavern Club, taking in all Fab Four references along the way ➤**Aintree Racecourse The Grand National Experience** (0151 522 2921) The world-famous steeplechase and its sumptuous facilities, including the mythical Red Rum's grave and Aintree Museum ➤**Everton FC Tour** (0151 330 2277) Award-winning tour that lasts for over one hour ➤**Liverpool FC Museum & Tour Centre** (0151 260 6677) Highlights include five huge European Cups, 60-seat cinema and re-creation of the famous standing Spion Kop.

DECEMBER 2007

150th anniversary of first game of Liverpool Rugby Club - World's First Open Rugby Union Club.

Dyingfrog Artworks
Across the city
December

Photographs of Liverpool. Also online at www.dyingfrog.co.uk/i-saw

Winter Celebration
Court Hey Park and National Wildflower Centre, Knowsley
Sunday 2 December 12.00 to 4.30pm

An opportunity to take part in winter crafts, stock up on Christmas presents from the craft fair and shop and enjoy seasonal food and entertainment.

The Liverpool Nativity
Sunday 16 December. Free

Performed live and in public on the streets of Merseyside and broadcast live on BBC Three, the ultimate nativity for Christmas 2007.

Emilia di Liverpool
European Opera Centre
St George's Hall,
Small Concert Room
From Monday 31 December

A new version of Emilia di Liverpool drawn from the 1824 and 1828 editions. Director Elisabeth Linton (Sweden) and conductor Giovanni Pacor (Italy) aim to make 'Emilia'a theatrical experience for contemporary audiences.

New Year's Eve Fireworks Show
Monday 31 December

Liverpool will be illuminated by a spectacular series of simultaneous events housed in venues old and new and animating public spaces throughout the city. Liverpool waves goodbye to 2007 and says hello to its future as a European Capital of Culture.

AN EXTRA 1.7MILLION VISITORS BY 2008
Good job, then, there's lots of great places to stay...

Budget or boutique? Economy or indulgence? The quantity and quality of a city's hotels is a fair indication of its stature, and Liverpool is now spoilt for choice. The city centre offers old favourites and unique newcomers, with a cluster of affordable options around Lime Street. The waterfront boasts a baker's dozen ranging from spectacular developments to express hotels around Albert Dock. Good job, too, with overseas visits doubling for Liverpool's 800th birthday and the city up from 16th to sixth in the visitor league.

Opening its doors on Princes Dock in 2007 is Malmaison, one of the hippest hotel chains around, and the proposed New World Square promises an international hotel adjacent to the new cruise-liner facility. No62 Castle Street is a £2.5million renovation of the former Trials Hotel that's resulted in a contemporary finish complementing the elegant exterior. Hope Street Hotel, meanwhile, has received planning permission to double in size, and the old Gladstone on Lord Nelson Street has completed its own £6.5million makeover to become the Liner at Liverpool. And check out the revamped Blackburne Arms – now a boutique hotel – on the corner of Catharine Street and Falkner Street.

Hard Day's Night, at the corner of South John Street and Mathew Street, will be the world's first Beatles-themed boutique hotel with 110 bedrooms each telling a different part of the Fab Four story through original artwork by Beatles artist Shannon. Hilton are opening a hotel in the new crescent-shaped block at Canning Place, part of Grosvenor's Liverpool One project, and the nearby King's Waterfront will boast a Jurys Inn and Stalybridge Hotel.

Hard to believe that the Radisson SAS on Old Hall Street will be three years old in 2007. It's since been joined by the classy Sir Thomas Hotel with its footballer-friendly bar at the corner of Victoria Street and Sir Thomas Street. The Racquet Club on Chapel Street continues to attract A-list faces, while the Crowne Plaza, Marriott and Thistle are corporate stalwarts. Not forgetting those Liverpool institutions, the Adelphi and Holiday Inn.

Racquet Club, Chapel Street

Malmaison Hotel, Princes Dock

Sir Thomas Street Hotel

READY TO ORDER
The best cuisine in Liverpool.
From around the world with love...

Whatever you want to eat, you'll find it in a city whose variety of cuisine reflects its rich multi-cultural heritage. There are the aesthetics of dining-out to consider, too. Choose modern British cooking in minimalist steel-and-glass venues on the waterfront, authentic Russian food in the raucous environs of Rope Walks, sophisticated international cuisine in the city's theatreland, and just about everything in-between. There are good modern venues at Queen Square, a stretch of fabulous establishments in the Hope Quarter, and numerous lounge-bar options around the Business District and Albert Dock. And that's not including all the dim-sum delights of Chinatown and abundance of cool cafés all over town. Or, for that matter, some great European-style delicatessens.

Room restaurant at 62 Castle Street

Decisions decisions...

➤ ROOM (62 Castle Street) award-winning restaurant serving up retro British food and creative cocktails

➤ ABOVE & BELOW (Wood Street) modern eclectic global cuisine and a basement bar

➤ HEART AND SOUL (Mount Pleasant) 'food, music and love' in a beautifully-restored Georgian merchant's house

➤ LONDON CARRIAGE WORKS (Hope Street Hotel) aiming for Michelin status by 2008

➤ 60 HOPE STREET (Hope Street) destination restaurant in the truest sense, with classy cooking in a discrete but unstuffy setting

➤ SIMPLY HEATHCOTES (Beetham Plaza) modern British cuisine at its best

➤ ZIBA at RACQUET CLUB (Chapel Street) located in Liverpool's premier boutique hotel

➤ PUSCHKA (Rodney Street) bistro and outstanding example of How To Get It Right

➤ FILINI at RADISSON SAS (Old Hall Street) inspired by the best of Sardinian cuisine with an exclusively Italian wine list

➤ IL FORNO (Duke Street) opened in 2005 as Liverpool's 'first authentic Italian restaurant'

➤ SAPPORO TEPPANYAKI (Duke Street) sushi and noddle café-bar praised for its 'variety of food, eating experience and general ambience'

➤ MEET (Brunswick Street) Argentinian steakhouse with tasty portions and excellent service

WHERE THE ART IS

Eight centuries all add up to a fabulous artistic legacy...

Main hall, Lady Lever Art Gallery

Not so long ago Sir Jeremy Isaacs gave a speech at FACT. The former director general of the Royal Opera House was also chairman of the judging panel that had chosen Liverpool as European Capital of Culture for 2008. "Without question," he told a full house, "this city has the greatest single conglomeration of galleries and museums of any city outside London – and that is a very strong calling card indeed."

The jewel in the crown is National Museums Liverpool (NML), awarded the Freedom of Liverpool in 2004 and the collective name for the seven museums and galleries that make up the greatest collection of artefacts, paintings and specimens collectively held under single ownership in the country. They are: the National Conservation Centre, Lady Lever Art Gallery, World Museum Liverpool, Merseyside Maritime Museum and HM Customs & Excise National Museum, Sudley House and the Walker Art Gallery.

Since they became free to visit five years ago, the venues have attracted one million extra visitors per year – a 138 per cent increase and the biggest rise for any of the UK's attractions that scrapped entrances charges. Coming in 2007 is the International Slavery Museum at the Albert Dock, followed by the new Museum of Liverpool on the Pier Head.

Maritime Museum

NML is counterpointed by the streetwise fluidity of the Independents District. In this former 'shipping streets' area, organisations like the A Foundation, loveliverpool and the Picket contribute to a rich cultural offer, the jumbling and juxtaposition of the venerable with the modern making for a special mix. Greenland Street is a major new contemporary art centre just off Jamaica Street (opposite Cains Brewery).

Launched by A Foundation, it consists of three former industrial buildings (the Furnace, Blade Factory and Coach Shed) in the heart of the old port and up-and-coming cultural district, that have been transformed into 2,500sq metres of high-quality exhibition space for large-scale, experimental projects. It's also become the permanent venue for the judging of the John Moores 24 (art competition).

Then there's the Liverpool Biennial of Contemporary Art, a ten week celebration of the freshest and most innovative aspects of visual culture, in which several hundred of the world's most exciting artists show their work in over 40 locations across the city centre, from major gallery spaces to unexpected temporary locations.

It comprises the International (specially-commissioned works from around the world), the Independent (a celebration of eclectic works by acclaimed local, British and international artists), the John Moores 24 (the largest contemporary painting competition in the entire country, shortlisted by serious star names) and the Bloomburg New Contemporaries (art-school showcase inaugurating a brand new venue on Greenland Street, off Jamaica Street, in 2006).➤

➤ National Conservation Centre ➤
Whitechapel (0151) 478 4999
Visit: conservationcentre.org.uk
Awards galore for the UK's first national conservation centre, housed in a Victorian goods office and just refurbished to the tune of £1million. It leads the way in laser-cleaning (to remove surface layers of dirt from statues) and 3D digital scanning (to produce highly accurate replicas replacing original works threatened with further damage). The female personification of Liverpool, once on the roof of the Walker and now in the Centre's foyer, is the perfect example.

Clockwise from right: National Conservation Centre, World Museum Liverpool, Walker Art Gallery, Maritime Museum, Lady Lever Art Gallery

Lady Lever Art Gallery ▲
Port Sunlight Village (0151) 478 4136
Over the water for the collected art treasures of Edwardian philanthropist and soap magnate, William Hesketh Lever. Currently showing Merchant Palaces, a photographic celebration of the lost interiors of Liverpool's grand Victorian houses, to celebrate the Year of Heritage, and later in 2007 the work of Belgian artist James Ensor. The gallery also has memorabilia relating to Lever's fascination with Napoleon.

Merseyside Maritime Museum ▲ and HM Customs & Excise National Museum
Albert Dock (0151) 478 4499
Tells the story of one of the world's greatest ports and the people who used it. Find out what it felt like to cross mighty oceans as an emigrant or a slave. Experience the palatial world of liners like the Titanic and Lusitania. And explore the history of smuggling since the 1700s. Four floors of exhibitions reflecting Liverpool's seafaring heritage.

◀ World Museum Liverpool
William Brown Street (0151) 478 4399

One of the country's premier museums, now boasting a stunning extension with a six-storey, glass-topped atrium. Re-opened in spring 2004 after a £35million expansion that's doubled its size and allowed thousands of fascinating artefacts to go on show for the first time in 50 years.

The new wing is beautifully designed and fully interactive, with six floors, a theatre, café and lots of places to play and rest. Don't miss (as if you can) the dinosaurs, giant creepie-crawlies that spring into life when you get close, African tribal masks, ancient Egyptian tombstones, native American head dresses and fabulous aquarium. If it's out there, it's in here.

Sudley House ▼
Mossley Hill Road (0151) 724 3245

The former home of wealthy Victorian ship-owner George Holt re-opens to the public this summer, showcasing masterpieces by Gainsborough, Turner, and the Pre-Raphaelites in all their glory.

The Walker ▲
William Brown Street (0151) 478 4199

The first British public art gallery and one of the finest in Europe. The full-length Henry VIII portrait is thought to have belonged to his favourite wife Jane Seymour, while William Hogarth's 1745 painting of David Garrick as Richard III captures the Marlon Brando of his day in full method-acting mode.

John Brett's The Stonebreaker is the favourite painting of Sir Peter Blake (designer behind the Beatles Sgt Pepper album cover), who calls it "a tiny, jewel-like painting among a superb collection." And the Tinted Venus, whose flesh-coloured body, blue eyes and golden hair caused a scandal when she was shown in London in 1862, is the beloved creation of local neo-classical sculptor John Gibson. He was loathe to give her up, writing to the wife of the rich Liverpool patron who commissioned him: "It would be as difficult for me to part with her as it would be for your husband to part with you." Have we mentioned the Rubens, Rembrandt, Seurat, Cezanne, Poussin, Degas, Freud, Hockney, Gilbert and George?

Bluecoat Arts Centre/Display Centre ➤
School Lane/Hanover Street (0151) 709 5297

The Grade I listed cornerstone of Liverpool's artistic life, its studios, stages, workshops and galleries newly refurbished for 2007, its tree-lined courtyard complemented by a new wing housing a gallery and performance space. The city centre's oldest building – and arguably its most elegant – was founded by a sea captain in 1717. With a continuous programme of innovative exhibitions and events, BAC has pioneered the visual and performing arts for decades, while Bluecoat Display Centre is consistently nominated as one of the best contemporary applied arts centres outside London.

FACT ▼
88 Wood Street (0151) 707 4450

As in, Foundation for Arts and Creative Technology. It opened its sliding doors in 2003 as Liverpool's 'arts project for the digital age' (the first new building dedicated to the arts since the Philharmonic Hall in 1939). Inside the £11million complex, you'll find two galleries dedicated to new media artwork, and three state-of-the-art cinemas showing arthouse and mainstream movies. There's a dinky clubhouse for hire called The Box, plus cafés and bars with great views across the Liverpool cityscape. It's an unparalleled support system for UK artists and another icon of Liverpool's cultural renaissance.

Tate Liverpool ▲
Albert Dock (0151) 702 7400

Otherwise known as the National Collection of Modern Art in the North of England, it will celebrate its 20th birthday in 2008 and recently welcomed its ten millionth visitor. Around 600,000 visitors a year admire its works from the Tate Collection and special exhibitions of contemporary art – making it the most visited modern art gallery outside London. Picasso, Cezanne, Matisse, Pollock, Warhol, and Jake and Dinos Chapman have all starred, and even its café even has a specially-commissioned, three-dimensional installation. It was the first gallery in the UK to pioneer the use of information assistants. With a global reputation, you'd be mad to miss it.

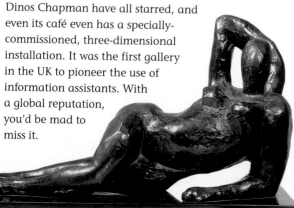

Exhibition at the University's Art Gallery

Central Library and Record ▲

Office William Brown Street
Tel: (0151) 233 5835

Its Picton Reading Room is a work of art in itself. From February to June 2007, the original 1207 document and originals and copies of the 23 key royal charters granted to the City of Liverpool from medieval times onwards, all of which are held and cared for by Liverpool Record Office, will go on display.

Also on show will be medieval deeds, 18th century maps, copies of watercolours and photographs, the city's first directory of 1766 and Liverpool bank notes from the 1790s. Don't miss John James Audubon's magnificent Birds of America book and the equally rare volumes in the Hornby Library and Oak Room.

The Record Office's photographic collections have just been awarded 'designation status' (highly prestigious) by the Museums, Libraries & Archives Council.

59 Rodney Street

(0151) 709 6261

Home to Edward Chambré Hardman Photographic Collection, where the entire lifetime output – in excess of 142,000 images – of an internationally renowned photographer are in the process of being catalogued, digitised, conserved and made accessible to view in his former studio, offering a unique insight into Liverpool and its people. The venue is a typically elegant Georgian terraced house, opened to the public by the National Trust.

Liverpool Academy of Arts

36 Seel Street (0151) 709 0735

Dating back to 1763, the LAA is currently a small gallery dedicated to local artists, with an annual Beatles Art exhibition (last week in July to first in September).

University of Liverpool Art Gallery ▲

6 Abercromby Square (0151) 794 2348

Works by Turner, Epstein and Freud, plus American wildlife artist JJ Audubon, all displayed in a beautiful Georgian terrace house. In 2008 it'll be transferred to the university's Victoria Building, undergoing a £7.5million conversion to hold the collections.

Much of the items on display will never have been on public view before. Highlights include a glass passenger lift within the clock tower, and a remodelled entrance at the east end of the building.

Open Eye Gallery

28-32 Wood Street (0151) 709 9460

Long-established, much-loved and showcasing innovative and challenging photography and media art with an international pedigree, including many world premieres and talks by the artists themselves. From abstract and detached images of the modern world to the power of the veil in Islamic society.

View Two Gallery

23 Mathew Street (0151) 236 9444

Three floors of wonderfully eclectic work by local and global artists in an informal venue on Liverpool's 'Carnaby Street'. There's a licensed bar, too, though staff will be just as happy to make you a cup of tea.

Western Approaches Museum

1-3 Rumford Street (0151) 227 2008

A permanent reminder of Liverpool's role as Area Command HQ for the Battle of the Atlantic. Eerie, underground, awe-inspiring.

Stained glass, Ullet Road Unitarian Church

Penelope, Wolstenholme Square

ART FOR EVERYONE

"A poetic response to individual and universal sentiments associated with emigration – sadness at leaving but the hope of a new future in another place." That's how Antony Gormley characterised his 100 cast-iron sculptures spread out across 3km of Crosby Beach.

On a far smaller scale, conceptual artist Tracey Emin unveiled her own gift to Liverpool ("one of my favourite cities") and her first piece of public art, with her own rarefied explanation: "Birds are the angels of this earth and they represent freedom." Called 'Roman Standard' and inspired by the Liver Bird, it takes the form of a bronze sparrow-like bird atop a four-metre high pole, and it's behind the Oratory gates next to the Liverpool Cathedral.

"It represents strength but also femininity," she adds. "Most public sculptures are a symbol of power which I find oppressive and dark. I wanted something that had a magic and an alchemy, something which would appear and disappear and not dominate."

Emin's public art followed other new arrivals in the city like 'Penelope', the twisting, glowing steel sculpture in Wolstenholme Square by Cuban artist Jorge Pardo (a reference to both Liverpool's maritime past and the unshakable faith of Ulysses' wife in the ancient Greek myth) and the 'Faces of Liverpool' in blue glass portholes around Beetham Tower (celebrating the city's global connections and diverse culture with images of its contemporary residents).

Among the best post-war public sculptures are the Piazza Waterfall at Beetham Plaza designed by Richard Huws to recreate the sound and fury of 'the restless, temperamental sea', and Charlotte Mayer's 'Sea Circle' 'reflecting the constant coming and going of men, women and ships to and from this great port'. Other landmarks include 'The Great Escape', Edward Cronshaw's bronze sculpture of a man restraining a horse made of unravelling rope, and 'A Case History', John King's stack of luggage piled on Hope Street's pavement for the city's first Biennial in 1998.

The same year, 'SuperLambBanana' (now relocated to Tithebarn Street from Wapping) was created by Japanese artist Taro Chiezo as a parody of genetic engineering. Seek out, too, older gems like the stained-glass window by Edward Burne-Jones and William Morris, in Ullet Road Unitarian Church just off Sefton Park in south Liverpool, and the Art Nouveau gates of the Philharmonic Hotel that rival anything by Gaudi and the Modernists in Barcelona.➤

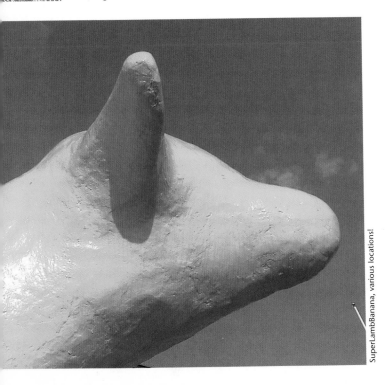

SuperLambBanana, various locations!

➤Excitingly, more and more art is appearing in Liverpool's bars and restaurants – and on the streets themselves (like the Slater Street graffiti by the world-renowned Banksy). We urge you to view the murals of radical Liverpudlians by David Jacques in the Newz Bar (Water Street), Anthony Brown's portraits and cityscapes in Colin's Bridewell and the Radisson SAS hotel, and the fabulous and often very famous works hanging in top restaurant 60 Hope Street. The Biennial always appropriates the public landscape, and of late construction sites have been converted into outdoor galleries to both engage the public and chronicle the city's current eye-catching renaissance.

© Anthony Brown

A Case History, Hope Street

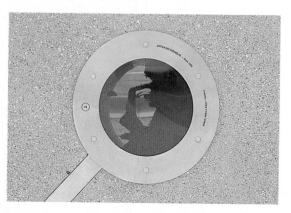

Faces of Liverpool, Beetham Tower complex

Michaelangelo outside the Walker

CAPITAL OF SCULPTURE

Take a look around, it's everywhere

Only London surpasses Liverpool for public sculpture in the UK. The city is a microcosm of British taste in this most accessible of art forms: from the conventional bronze 'portrait' statues of Victorian times, like the Wellington Column on William Brown Street, when thousands of people would turn out for the unveiling ceremonies; to the more symbolic decoration in the early 20th Century, such as the Cenotaph at St George's Plateau.

There used to be more. Precisely because so much sculpture is displayed outdoors, away from the protective environment of a museum or gallery, it's at risk. What's left in Liverpool today – 150 monuments,

not including the many busts from mythology lining the streets like ancient sentinels – is only what's survived time, pollution, demolition, coastal weather and wartime bombing over the last 200 years.

The award-winning National Conservation Centre near Queen Square has helped to reverse the trend, leading the way in laser-cleaning and 3D digital scanning. It has restored George Frampton's much-loved statue of Peter Pan and returned it to Sefton Park, and on permanent display in its foyer is the sculpture of Eros that also stood in the park.

One of the first statues to be replaced in recent times was the female personification of Liverpool on the roof of the Walker. The original marble figure by John Warrington Wood (he also did the Michelangelo and Raphael outside the gallery) was carved in Rome, shipped to Liverpool and erected here in 1877. It epitomises an era when local sculptors, many of whom studied in Italy, were patronised by 'merchant princes' keen to leave their mark for posterity. It was replaced by a replica from China in 1993 and now stands in the National Conservation Centre.

After the Victorian obsession with civic pride came an explosion of rich and freely expressive architectural decoration, from the Monument to the Engine Room Heroes on the Pier Head to the stylised carvings on the George's Dock Building – collectively known as 'the New Sculpture', often executed by graduates from the city's School of Architecture, and a bridge to the modern era signified by Jacob Epstein's Liverpool Resurgent (above Lewis's).

Liverpool Resurgent, by Jacob Epstein, Lewis's department store

PLACE THE FACES

(Right) clockwise from top left: Hope Street Hotel, Adelphi Hotel x 2, No1 Dale Street (Royal Bank of Scotland), Cunard Building (Pier Head) x 2, George's Dock Building (Pier Head), Cunard Building x 2, Blackburne House (Hope Street), No1 Dale Street, Athenaeum (Church Alley), Cunard Building x 2, Metropolitan Cathedral of Christ, JMU Hahnemann Hospital (Hope Street), University Ashton Building (Brownlow Hill), Paradise Street Power Station.

Liverpool personified, roof of Walker

Steble Fountain, William Brown Street

PERFORMANCE

From gripping drama and beautiful ballet to gag factories
and funky urban sounds. That's entertainment...

Live theatre in Liverpool is back and buzzing, with the Everyman and Playhouse under the dynamic leadership of directors Gemma Bodinetz and Deborah Aydon.

Specialising in bold interpretations of the very best drama, the Playhouse is the UK's oldest established repertory company. The Everyman has a reputation for staging ground-breaking work from the most talented directors, writers and actors in the business. It's produced stars like Julie Walters, Bill Nighy, Jonathan Pryce and Peter Postlethwaite, and playwrights like Willy Russell, Alan Bleasdale and Jimmy McGovern. In 2005 it had a star-studded 40th birthday party, and launched a new programme of 'Made in Liverpool' productions complemented by some of the best touring work around. 'Unprotected', which premiered at the Everyman in 2006, won rave reviews at the Edinburgh Festival Fringe followed by several awards.

But there's more to these theatres than simply the work on their stages. A busy literary department nurtures the next generation of Liverpool playwrights, while a community department takes their work to all corners of the city, in partnership with schools, colleges, youth and community groups to open up the theatres to all. The Everyman and Playhouse are the city's major employer of theatre artists, artisans and skilled support staff.

Deborah Aydon and Gemma Bodinetz

An adventurous programme has found an enthusiastic audience displaying a fabulous degree of loyalty to the theatres, with attendances growing significantly and an extensive programme of commissioning and playwright support nurturing local artists and sowing the seeds of the future.

Among the many highlights planned for 2008, tributes to Liverpool institutions Eric's club and the Adelphi Hotel, and an exciting new adaptation of King Lear. Next up, proposals to redevelop the theatres with the addition of new facilities. Key elements, scheduled to begin in 2009, include: a new Everyman which has at its heart the dynamic and democratic 'thrust' configuration which has inspired artists and audiences; refurbishment of the Grade II listed Playhouse to bring out its heritage character while equipping for its future; shared-used studio theatre for small-scale productions of cutting-edge new work, work space for the growing stable of Liverpool writers, new backstage facilities and office space for the staff. Grand total: £35million.

The aim is for these theatres to be an engine for creative excellence, artistic adventure, and audience involvement – firmly rooted in the community, yet both national and international in scope and ambition.

➤ Liverpool Everyman Hope Street (0151) 708 4776
Liverpool Playhouse Williamson Square
(0151) 709 4776

Dance at the Everyman-Playhouse

Liverpool Empire Theatre

Lime Street (0151) 708 3200

Set to stage the Royal Variety Performance in 2007, the UK's largest two-tiered theatre is a visual treat, all velvet seats, gilded décor, brocaded curtains and dizzyingly high ceiling. Only the Albert Hall can hold a candle to this stunning venue, recently refurbished and now just as grand with state-of-the-art facilities.

Its 2006 programme included Ellen Kent with Grigorovich's Nutcracker, My Fair Lady, and three outstanding shows from Welsh National Opera (The Flying Dutchman, Jephtha and The Marriage of Figaro). Whatever the show, at night there's a sensational view from the lounge bar across to St George's Hall and William Brown Street. Sublime.

Music at the Philharmonic Hall

Philharmonic Hall

Hope Street (0151) 709 3789

Home to the Royal Liverpool Philharmonic Orchestra – one of Europe's oldest – and so much more. There's a youth orchestra and gospel choir, and the hall regularly hosts gigs and world music concerts (from Bacharach to Buena Vista) plus audiences with intellectuals and raconteurs.

The building itself has been called 'frozen music' – designed by the great Herbert Rowse to fuse modernist style with acoustic data (after the original hall's fire in 1933).

He described it as "shaped like a megaphone with the orchestra at the narrow end." Inside, there are etched-glass decorations, gilded reliefs of Apollo and a memorial to the musicians of the Titanic. Rowse's initials, it's claimed, are woven into the sumptuous carpets.

Once you've admired the décor's riot of musical motifs, close your eyes and let some of the world's best musicians serenade you. The Phil's intimate Rodewall Suite hosts After Eight, a series of informal roots and jazz gigs – ideal for hearing world-class performances with a pint in your hand.

Have we mentioned the movies yet? Classic Films at the Phil features everything from the Parisian splendour of Moulin Rouge to the hard-boiled noir of the Coen brothers, shown on the world's only surviving Walturdaw cinema screen. What's one of those?

A screen with a proscenium that's raised through the stage via a system of antique counterweights. That's what. ➤

Neptune Theatre

Hanover Street (0151) 709 7844

An intimate venue, which will be refurbished for 2008, whose shows vary from classic drama to dance to children's plays. There are regular clairvoyant and murder-mystery nights.

Unity Theatre

1 Hope Place (0151) 709 4988

On the site of a synagogue and one of a select group of UK venues formed before World War II 'to make theatres accessible to the great mass of the people'. It's maintained its reputation for staging innovative, adventurous work and showcases rising talent from LIPA. There's children's theatre, too, plus a commitment to major city events (Writing on the Wall, Liverpool Comedy Festival etc). Patrons include actors Cathy Tyson, Ian Hart and Alison Steadman.

Liverpool Institute for Performing Arts

Mount Street (0151) 709 4988

Tomorrow's stars today – for example, former graduate and singer-songwriter Sandi Thom. LIPA runs two seasons of public productions (dance, drama and musicals) each year with students performing in up to 30 shows in the Paul McCartney Auditorium and Sennheiser Studio Theatre – watch out for their evenings of show-stopping jazz.

Flamenco at the Neptune

Beauty and the Beast at the Unity

LIPA's Outburst in performance

JUST THE GIG

Watch out for the forthcoming Arena and Convention Centre Liverpool on Kings Waterfront, set to hold major concerts for up to 10,000 spectators by 2008.

As it is, the Carling Academy on Hotham Street is a rocking joint just around the corner from Lime Street and the Empire Theatre (on the site of the old Lomax). The main auditorium holds 1,200 and hosts legends and upstarts in equal measure. The 500-capacity Academy 2 showcases rising talent, while Subculture is two rooms of rock and alternative music with guest deejays. The university's Academy on Mount Pleasant, meanwhile, is three venues in one, while the Royal Court on Roe Street is back to its best as a headliner music venue (when it's not staging phenomenally successful plays like Brick Up The Mersey tunnels). Not forgetting 3345 Parr Street, the famous recording studio complex that's been used by the likes of Coldplay, Embrace and Badly Drawn Boy.

Zanzibar on Seel Street is smaller than most but perfectly formed, and great for rising local talent and catching the next big thing. There are more informal gigs – often by true superstars – at the likes of Korova (Wood Street), Residents Lounge (Hope Street Hotel), Pan American (Albert Dock) and the Living Room (Victoria Street).

Where to start with Liverpool's throbbing club scene? The Masque on Seel Street is Liverpool's streetwise shack and the epicentre of Liverpool's urban music scene. Cheeky, trashy, funky, and all facilitated by the tastiest young turntable technicians.

Echo and the Bunnymen frontman Ian McCulloch during a solo performance

Coldplay and Liverpool, Parr Street producer Ken Nelson accept their Grammy Awards for "Clocks" album in 2004, in Los Angeles. (AP Photo/Kevork Djansezian)

Chibuku, four JMU graduates (named after a beer from Malawi) who started a monthly night at the Lemon Lounge on Berry Street, graduated here and are now regarded as one of the best underground nights in the country, attracting high-profile producers and deejays from LA to Ibiza.

Metropolitan on Berry Street is a bohemian bar run by the former manager of the famous Mello Mello Bar, with club nights upstairs at the Lemon Lounge. Over at Society on Duke Street, Friday resident Mike Da Scale is generally regarded as producing the best house in Liverpool right now, while Yousef is an internationally-acclaimed Liverpudlian deejay of Egyptian descent whose Circus night at the Masque has been named Radio One's Club of the Year. For R&B, head for Concert Square at weekends and Radio City deejay Spykatcha.

For top comedy, check out downstairs at the Laughterhouse on Fenwick Street, established for four years now as a centre of comedic excellence. Howard Marks has done a turn here and Mark Thomas has topped the bill in the past. Rawhide is the city's original stand-up show, based at the Royal Court, going strong for 12 years and toasting the release of its own DVD featuring local stand-ups like Chris Cairns, Brendan Riley, Simon Bligh and Steve Gribben.

Liverpool FC, kings of Europe in 2005

THE THRILLS

Liverpool loves its sport. The question is, do you prefer to watch or join in?

Where to start? Two football clubs with the kind of pedigree others pine for. If you know your history, Everton are the first football club in England to spend 100 years in the top flight – a feat celebrated in 2003 – and the one that's given the world two magnificent centre-forwards from different eras with the same world-class credentials. Dixie Dean was the first and only player to score 60 league goals in a season, back in 1928. Former Blue Wayne Rooney, now with Manchester United, surely has a host of records in front of him.

Everton FC, Homecoming 1985 After winning the League Championship, Cup Winners Cup, and Charity Shield

Anfield is one of the most legendary sporting venues on the planet, home of Liverpool FC and a shrine for hundreds of thousands of pilgrims worldwide. Outside is a statue of Bill Shankly, mythical manager in the Swinging Sixties. Both 'the Shanks' and successor Bob Paisley – the only coach to guide a team to three European Cup victories – are commemorated by giant gates either side of the stadium, which also has a Hillsborough Memorial.

The club's success on the pitch is unsurpassed: five European Cups, three UEFA Cups, three European Super Cups, a record 18 League Championships, seven FA Cups and seven League Cups. Many of the trophies are on show at the club museum, where you'll also experience the electric atmosphere of the old Spion Kop and learn about the Liverpool anthem You'll Never Walk Alone. A space-age 60,000-seater stadium is planned for the near future, so get up to the original Anfield while you still can.

St Helens, one of top rugby league teams in the world, play 13 miles away from Liverpool city centre at Knowsley Road. Waterloo is the rugby union club in Crosby that's produced internationals like Dick Greenwood, Ben Kay and Will Greenwood.

St.Helens Rugby League Challenge Cup winners party 2006

Liverpool Cricket Club, 200 years old in 2007, stages Lancashire CC fixtures and was a firm favourite with Don Bradman. For top-class tennis, see Calderstones Park. A glorious setting with 36 grass courts and a 5,000-seater stadium, in mid-June it hosts the Liverpool International Tennis Tournament, a Wimbledon warm-up with stars aplenty and a Legends event that's featured Martina Navratilova, among others.

There's the Grand National, no other horse race quite like it. Four miles and 856 yards that have 600million viewers glued to their TV sets all over the globe, with two huge grandstands and a new parade ring at Aintree. And Haydock Park, over 250 years old and one of the country's premier racecourses.

So many great golf courses – this is England's Golf Coast, remember – it's ever-so-slightly embarrassing, including some of the UK's most challenging and beautiful venues nestling between the pace of urban life and ruggedness of the coastline. Considered to be the best course in the country, Birkdale and its mighty

Yacht Race at Liverpool Marina

Aintee, where else?

sand dunes (near Southport) will stage the Open Championship for the ninth time in 2008. Royal Liverpool on Hoylake, of course, hosted the event in 2006.

Excellent sailing facilities come as standard. Liverpool Yacht Club is located in the Marina & Harbourside Club, half-a-nautical-mile from the scuba-diving centre at Albert Dock, with races every other weekend on the Mersey and out to the Irish Sea and regular day-trips along the beautiful coasts of North and West Wales, the Isle of Man, Cumbria and Scotland. Climbing? Awesome Walls Centre on Athol Street is one of the largest indoor climbing centres in Europe with walls and routes to suit all skill levels.

OUT OF TOWN

You are now 50 miles, as the Liver Bird flies, from the highest peak in Wales (Snowdon) and 65 miles from England's biggest mountain (Scafell Pike in the Lake District). In-between, there's rather a lot going on

Opposite the Pier Head is Birkenhead with its Norman Priory dating from 1150. Further north is Seacombe's Aquarium and new £8million Astronomy & Space Centre, then New Brighton. Head south for Port Sunlight Heritage Centre (Lady Lever Art Gallery and over 900 listed buildings and gardens) and Ellesmere Port's Boat Museum and Blue Planet Aquarium. The other side of Wirral boasts West Kirby Marine Lake, and Hilbre Islands Local Nature Reserve. Due south is Wirral Country Park in Thurstaston and the picturesque resort of Parkgate. From here you're a matter of minutes from the walled city of Chester, easily accessed on Merseyrail.

South along Riverside Drive from the city-centre is the serene promenade at Otterspool (and giant beech trees in the adjacent park), and later Halewood Triangle Country Park (the region's oldest native woodland) plus the National Trust splendour of Speke Hall. To the north-east there's Croxteth Hall &

Tiger at Knowsley Safari Park

Doctor Who Exhibition, Seacombe Spaceport on the Wirral

Southport's Lord Street

Country Park, an historic mansion in a wooded park, and Knowsley, home to the National Wildflower Centre and the Safari Park, the first of its kind to open by a large city and a haven for lions, tigers, elephants and rhino – and more than 50 baby animals born over a few weeks last summer.

Due north from Waterloo is the Sefton Coast with its string of nature reserves. Formby Point is the fourth largest dune system in the country and home to one of Britain's last colonies of red squirrels and natterjack toads, as well as a wonderful array of birdlife such as oystercatchers, sanderlings, yellowhammers and greater spotted woodpeckers.

On to the elegant seaside resort of Southport, approximately 20 miles from Liverpool, with golden sands, green lawns, Victorian shopping arcades and a climate that boasts more sunshine hours than anywhere else in the North West of England.

LIVERPOOL
1207~2007

OFFICIAL SOUVENIR

Cheshire Year of Gardens '08

Cheshire's Year of Gardens '08, a year long festival, will celebrate the rich heritage of the gardens and green environment in Cheshire. Few other areas of the UK can boast the range and number of superb gardens and horticultural excellence that can be found in this famously green-fingered county.

The year long programme will comprise of a wide range of cultural, garden based events and activities to link closely with the Liverpool Capital of Culture '08 and complement the urban based programme.

The project has been developed by a partnership of organisations, including Visit Chester & Cheshire (VCC) and Cheshire County Council with the support of Cheshire's leading gardens.

As well as providing benefits to the environment, local communities and a wide range of tourism related businesses, it will aim to ensure garden attractions enjoy a legacy of increased numbers of visitors, together with improved facilities, infrastructure and training. There are 23 gardens to explore.

Lyme Park

Ness Gardens

Arley Hall

Tatton Park In Cheshire

Ness Gardens

These outstanding botanic gardens overlooking the Dee Estuary contain the finest collection of rhododendrons and azaleas in the Northwest; one of the best-known heather gardens in Britain; and an outstanding collection of Himalayan and Chinese plants.

They also boast magnificent herbaceous borders, specimen shrubs and a herb garden containing all the major culinary herbs. A new state of the art Visitor Centre with gift shop, café and plant nursery welcomes you.

Tatton Park

Explore Tatton Park's 50 acres of award winning gardens, rated among the best in the country. Representing over 200 years of garden design and history, notable features include the renowned Japanese Garden, Italian Garden, one of Britain's finest ferneries, a scented rose garden, early arboretum and recently restored Walled Kitchen Garden.

REMEMBER WEDNESDAY 4 JUNE 2003?

The future of Liverpool changed forever...

Utter jubilation, bewildering excitement and tears of sheer pride when the city was awarded European Capital of Culture 2008. Culture secretary Tessa Jowell said: "Liverpool is a worthy winner." Sir Jeremy Isaacs: "Liverpool looked good, sounded good, feels good to be in and would deliver a really terrific year... The whole city is involved in the bid and behind the bid."

Over three years later, we're bang on course and about to embark, straight after the 800th birthday, on arguably the greatest, grandest, most momentous 12 months in Liverpool's incredible history. It's almost our time and it's very definitely our place. The world is watching and we're going to put on a breathtaking show. 2008 is just the start...

The year will be heralded by an outdoor Christmas Nativity of a scale and ambition the UK has not seen before – the story of the first Christmas told through the music and people of Liverpool, its streets transformed by a torchlight procession flowing in from all points towards a floodlit plaza for one spectacular exultation of civic pride.

The year 2008 will embrace the heritage of Liverpool's maritime roots in its every manifestation. Cities On the Edge is a year-long cultural linking of seven great European cities. Gdansk, Istanbul, Marseilles, Naples, Bremen and Stavanger share with Liverpool a waterfront setting on the edge of their countries, plus a passionate and irreverent nature. Over a million people are expected to watch the start of the Tall Ships' Races 2008 in July when over 100 vessels will grace this great port once again.

They'll be joined during the summer by the Round-the-World Clipper Yacht Race and the Honda F4 Powerboats Series in September.

The River Niger Orchestra from the Congo, performing traditional African folk songs

800
TH
LIVERPOOL
1207~2007

OFFICIAL SOUVENIR

Left: World Museum fun, cultural graffiti,
and street entertainer.
Below: another happy audience at the
Playhouse
Bottom: More celebrations
at Chinese New Year

There will be new commissions from the Everyman and Playhouse, including Adelphi – The Musical, an affectionate tribute to one of Liverpool's best-known landmarks. The theatres have also commissioned an adaptation of Chekhov's Three Sisters, relocating it from Russia to the Liverpool Jewish community of 1948, and they're in dialogue with Pete Postlethwaite to return as King Lear.

Not forgetting the Bluecoat's literature programme, Writing on the Wall, and the University of Liverpool's Shipping Lines Literary Festival. Guests will include Doris Lessing, Seamus Heaney, Monica Ali, Melvyn Bragg, Philip Pullman and Roger McGough. The city will also host the coveted Stirling Prize for Architecture.

Liverpool musical heritage runs through dozens of wonderful events – from the Everyman's new production of Eric's, a witty and inspirational tale of the Mathew Street underground club that sparked a cultural revolution – to NML's The Beat Goes On, tracing the city's role in the legacy of pop music. The Liverpool Sound is a once-in-a-lifetime concert – beamed live around the globe from a unique waterfront setting. Our 800-year-old port will ripple to some of the planet's greatest artists playing the music that it exported to the world.

Liverpool has also exported some of its favourite sons, and in 2008 they'll return with Sir Simon Rattle conducting our very own Philharmonic Orchestra.

Tate Liverpool's Gustav Klimt exhibition inspires the Phil's city-wide musical celebration of Viennese culture, also mirrored in the orchestra's European tour with conductor Vasily Petrenko, which takes in Vienna. Africa Oyé and the Liverpool Arabic Arts Festival promise a world-class line-up of musicians exploring the continent's influence on the city's music and culture.

The Biennial throws an international spotlight on the city with a festival even bigger and bolder than the previous four. Alongside, Pavilions enables the inner-city communities of Vauxhall, Garston and Kensington to show their art in awe-inspiring structures built by international architects.

Throughout January there will be an opportunity to view the Turner Prize at Tate Liverpool, while at the Walker the 25th John Moores Exhibition of Contemporary Painting celebrates its 50th anniversary. Edge Hill, the world's first railway station, will be transformed into an art gallery.➤

2008 WHAT'S IT ALL ABOUT

➤Greenland Street, at the heart of the old port area, already boasts some of the largest exhibition spaces for contemporary art in the UK.

The Liverpool Commissions will unpick the hidden stories and unusual spaces that shape the city's personality. In the crypt of the Metropolitan Cathedral is an overview of Le Corbusier's most important architectural work, while Ben Johnson's Liverpool Panorama will be unveiled at the Walker, which is also hosting Monet to Hopper: the Artist and the Railway, in April. In October, the Stirling Prize – the Oscars of British architecture – will be held at the newly-opened Arena and Convention Centre Liverpool and screened live on Channel 4.

Elsewhere, the University of Liverpool's refurbished Victoria Building is displaying art and artefacts acquired throughout its 100-year history, the reborn Bluecoat Arts Centre brings together some of the finest visual, performing and interdisciplinary arts, and

FACT welcomes the world premiere of artist Pipilotti Rist's first feature film, Pepperminta.

Festivals of the world include Milapfest (South Asian), the Liverpool Arabic Arts Festival, Africa Oyé, Brouhaha International and the Liverpool Irish Festival. HUB provides a focal point for a riot of street arts – skateboarding, trick-cycling, street art and music. Mathew Street Music Festival and the Summer Pops will rise to the challenge of 2008, with Homotopia building upon its Queer New World programme.

Driven for and by the people, Creative Communities is putting culture at the heart of Liverpool's emotional regeneration as the largest programme of community arts in Europe. Chinese New Year will be celebrated with a Festival of Light from Beijing and Shanghai, and the August launch of the Black Star Liner will see Liverpool's first dedicated home for black music and a month of festivities in and around its Jamaica Street home.

Among a treasury of sporting moments, the image of Steven Gerrard lifting the Champions League trophy in Istanbul encapsulates the same passion that brought European Capital of Culture status to the city. In 2008 the sporting programme brings the world to Liverpool, and beams Liverpool back to the world.

The Open Golf Championship is at Royal Birkdale in July. Cycling's Tour of Britain will conclude here in September – the first time it's finished outside London. In March the Arena and Convention Centre Liverpool hosts the European Seniors Boxing Championship. In August, it's the World Firefighter Games.

The Liverpool International Tennis Tournament returns to Calderstones Park, and the Grand National enjoys an extra-special festival year at Aintree. There will also be a specially-commissioned performance by composer Michael Nyman that explores the intense pleasure and pain of European football culture, including a memorial to Hillsborough.

On a lighter note, the finale is a piece of music called Extra Time – performed by a brass band with footballers' wives and girlfriends hitting the catwalk dressed by Cricket.

GET INVOLVED!

Now is your chance to play a part in the greatest show on earth. Join the festivities and log onto liverpool08.com to become a Volunteer, sign up as an 08 Ambassador or join the thousands of local people shaping the city's cultural life through the Creative Communities Programme. Businesses, too, can play a part by signing up to the free-to-join 08businessconnect.com. Visit liverpool08.com, call (0151) 233 2008 or pop into the 08 Place at Whitechapel.